They Want To Help Us

Phenomenal True-Life Accounts Of The Unexplainable

50 SOURCES.
IN THEIR OWN WORDS.
REVEAL FOR THE FIRST TIME
100 TRUE-LIFE MIRACULOUS SPIRIT ACCOUNTS.

THOM BIERDZ

Copyright © 2019 Thom Bierdz Inc

All rights reserved.

ISBN:
978-1-7327320-7-0

DEDICATION

To the open hearts. To the open eyes. To the open souls.

CHAPTER 1	ON 9/10 I SAW SPIRIT RESCUES FOR 9/11		9
CHAPTER 2	WHY I COULDN'T FIND MY SPIRIT GUIDES THE WEEK OF 9/11		14
CHAPTER 3	SMELL OF DEATH FLOWERS: PLANE CRASH IN 1975		16
CHAPTER 4	CHEROKEE'S CHRISTMAS MESSAGE FROM SISTER		22
CHAPTER 5	A TENNIS PRO'S DEATH AND MIRACULOUS RETURN		28
CHAPTER 6	HOW DO I TELL ACEY WHEN HE WILL DIE?		31
CHAPTER 7	MY ONGOING RELATIONSHIP WITH THE DEAD		35
CHAPTER 8	PARENTS DANCING BETWEEN DIMENSIONS		43
CHAPTER 9	LEAVING HER BODY DURING MOLESTATION		46
CHAPTER 10	BOY GETS NIGHTLY ADVICE FROM GRANDMA'S GHOST		52
CHAPTER 11	EERILY ESCAPING DISASTER AFTER DISASTER		55
CHAPTER 12	GRANDMOTHER CROSSED THE LINE, LITERALLY		56
CHAPTER 13	PAPA AS MY RECURRING GUARDIAN ANGEL		57
CHAPTER 14	DEAD FATHER FINDS THEM A PERFECT APARTMENT		62
CHAPTER 15	TOMATO-LOVING FATHER DIES, LEAVES A SURPRISE		64
CHAPTER 16	HAUNTED HOUSE TURNS ON NEW OWNERS		67
CHAPTER 17	AN EMPATHETIC CHOKING		70
CHAPTER 18	ORGANIZED GROUP OF 12 SPIRITS: DIAGRAM INCLUDED		73
CHAPTER 19	RADIO AFFIRMS A MESSAGE FROM BEYOND		78
CHAPTER 20	RAINY SCOTLAND: ANOTHER COUNTRY & DIMENSION		80
CHAPTER 21	BRINGING BOOKS TO A MUTE GIRL IN THE ATTIC		84
CHAPTER 22	MOTHER-IN-LAW'S VOICE WARNING OF DANGER		86
CHAPTER 23	SECRET LOVE BROKEN: VOICE THAT CAN'T BE SILENCED		88
CHAPTER 24	READING MY MIND BENEATH A TEMPLE IN THAILAND		100
CHAPTER 25	SPIRIT GUIDES EXPLAINED & EERIE CRIMINAL BOND		103
CHAPTER 26	GRAMPA'S GHOST		112
CHAPTER 27	CHILDHOOD HABIT OF LEAVING MY BODY		114

CHAPTER 28	DOUSING	117
CHAPTER 29	A CROSS APPEARS ON THE CEILING	118
CHAPTER 30	BLOWN AWAY BY A PSYCHIC	119
CHAPTER 31	OF BROKEN WINGS	121
CHAPTER 32	MY DAD IS SET FREE	124
CHAPTER 33	400 LB. MAN MAKES EERIE PRESENCE KNOWN	126
CHAPTER 34	THE GHOST WITH FALSE TEETH	128
CHAPTER 35	MOMMY, THAT WAS THE MAN IN MY ROOM	129
CHAPTER 36	POP POP APPEARS OUT OF NOWHERE	131
CHAPTER 37	GRANDFATHER'S CHAIR	133
CHAPTER 38	TOUCHED BY AN ANGEL	134
CHAPTER 39	NAGGED WITH FEELING SOMEONE NEEDS RESCUE	136
CHAPTER 40	UNEXPLAINABLE SCREAMING	139
CHAPTER 41	A MAGIC GOURD FROM DAD?	141
CHAPTER 42	INVISIBLE HAND SAVES MY LIFE	144
CHAPTER 43	DOES NOT LIKE TALKING ABOUT THE GHOST	145
CHAPTER 44	HOPING FOR MOM BUT GRANDMA COMES	146
CHAPTER 45	GHOST VOICE TELLS ME TO LOCK MY CAR	148
CHAPTER 46	MUSEUM SCHOLAR SEES A NOVA SCOTIA PIRATE SHIP	149
CHAPTER 47	CLOSING A PORTAL TO THE OTHER SIDE	155
CHAPTER 48	I KNEW SHE WOULD DIE ON OCTOBER 17	157
CHAPTER 49	A VOICE SAYS NOT TO REMOVE MY TESTICLES	159
CHAPTER 50	CAN THE TODDLERS SEE THE DEAD MORE CLEARLY?	161
CHAPTER 51	MIRACULOUSLY SAVED FROM DEATH CRASH	163
CHAPTER 52	EXITING BANKING FOR A SPIRITUAL LIFE	166
CHAPTER 53	THOM BIERDZ'S OTHER PSYCHIC EXPERIENCES	168
CHAPTER 54	MY DEAD MOM DEMANDS I SEE TROY, HER KILLER	177

ACKNOWLEDGMENTS

While I do share my own spirit contact stories in the beginning and end of this exciting book, this is essentially only possible with the generous accounts given to me to give to you. Thank you all so very much for allowing me to share our spirit stories in one document. May we inspire a thousand more.

CHAPTER 1   ON 9/10 I SAW SPIRIT RESCUES FOR 9/11

by Thom Bierdz

This Wisconsin native, half-Italian, half-Polish, raised Catholic, a former soap opera star, now a fine-artist, is a skeptic when it comes to psychics. I don't believe most of the psychics I have been to in Los Angeles and I don't believe most the TV psychics either. They seem to guess in a way that they can't be wrong. I didn't believe James Von Praagh, until he told me exactly what I had asked to be voiced by him the day before our scheduled séance 25 years ago, before he was famous. I said to my dead mother the day before, "Mom, if this guy's for real, tell him to mention the blue and green frosting you used to put on my birthday cakes." James kept missing as he read me, guessing wrong things, and I was embarrassed for him, and he was sweating as the seven other people were already read and delighted by him, but I was the hard nut to crack. Sitting in my chair, arms crossed, legs crossed, I tried to hide the disappointment in my eyes. Finally, he said the words I asked to hear and my body relaxed. A breath of relief escaped my tightened face. My eyes were misty. He breathed, knowing he had reached the spirit world for me. The people in the room leaned in to hear why my mood had changed. I could barely get out the words to explain. Those words from him erased all doubt of my mother being "dead." James proved she was alive - somewhere. I know James Von Praagh is legit and he became world-famous soon after this. Maybe other TV psychics are, too. But I'm the type to not believe it until I see it for myself, or trust my intuition.

Still, I have been fortunate enough, and open enough, to have experienced some unexplainable phenomenon.

This account that follows is one experience that people told me for eighteen years to hush. They thought it would damage my credibility as an author and artist. But I can't keep it secret any longer. It is bigger than me. It needs to be told.

On a late summer evening in 2001 I lay in my Hollywood townhouse bed, under the covers, on my back. Next to me was my boyfriend Doug, an easy-going square-jawed waiter, and also in bed were our sleeping dogs, a Chihuahua and a Shepherd/Beagle. Even though I was allergic to dogs, I insisted we have them. They were like our kids and made Doug smile like never before. My hope was to get over my allergies, but, damn it, at that point I could not. My concerned Dad thought it was the craziest thing for me to challenge my nose and asthma by getting the dogs, but he was used to watching me go against the odds, challenge myself; challenge convention to be sure.

Dad was a patient man, a psychotherapist at one point, and didn't say too much. He listened more. He knew the diverse sides of me. He saw the rebel I was as a teenager, and also, ironically, the over-sensitive man I matured into, too. By that I don't mean I cried at movies, but at movies I would be aware of all those people around me in the theater seats, and their conversations. I paid more attention to their reaction to the movie than my reaction to the movie. That's just who I was; someone who seemed to be aware of everyone's conversations and body language, and someone trying to analyze people's small talk, even hours after they were gone. The puzzle of what they said and what they meant underneath it just stayed in my head, which probably has a correlation to why I paint in twenty different styles today; some very complicated disorientated pieces.

Anyway, back to lying in bed with Doug and the dogs. Over the years I had trained myself to "lucid-dream" at bedtime, meaning that when I closed my eyes I could see a myriad of disjointed symbols parading past my eyes - while I was fully awake.

Science says that the brain files the day away in symbols, not words; not pictures we'd recognize - so for years I trained myself to see these fascinating symbols form and dissolve into others. It was mind-boggling to be sure. For example, maybe a tomato would be a spinning top and inside a kite would appear and the kite would light up and dance and then an elephant's foot would be upside down and then striped in pinks and then a bicycle made of aluminum foil would be in the right corner of my still closed eyes view and then turn into a cane. I just use these examples of common symbols but in truth I only saw what had a personal meaning/subtext for me. These did not happen on a flat screen, per se, but were coming from all directions, at once sometimes. I don't remember the symbols I saw that particular night, or any other night, because they are so instantaneous and multifaceted. The books I read said this was "lucid-dreaming."

When these symbols first started - 10 years before - I tried to analyze what they meant but I couldn't keep up with their speed, and it was such an effort to watch/capture them and analyze each it exhausted me so eventually I stopped trying to figure out the meaning and just enjoy the show. A scientific book explained that these symbols were impossible to decipher with the conscious mind anyway, and not meant for the conscious mind - but meant for the subconscious mind.

How exciting for me that I had conscious access to my subconscious.

This was the most entertaining part of the day for me; like watching a bizarre, unpredictable movie while I was fully awake. After about ten minutes of this I would typically fall asleep and then I assume the symbols would continue as I entered the first stage of sleep.

But on this one unforgettable night, after only a minute into this fascinating parade of symbols did they came to an abrupt halt. This never happened before. Usually symbols layered on top of each other as the time progressed. Never had everything I was seeing just disappeared. I saw nothing - blackness - only blackness and stillness - which by its stagnancy meant that the lucid-dreaming was over. No question about it.

Yet I was still totally awake with my eyes closed, stuck, startled…waiting for who knows what. Then I saw something so horrible flash in front of my face that I remember needing to forget what I saw immediately. I have no idea what I saw. I only remember having to forget it! And I did forget it! This too, was uncharted behavior for me, as I had never tried so hard to forget anything in my life. Forgetting wasn't in my nature. I was the type to hang on to things and dwell on them, trying to decipher and analyze them, not the type to "need to" forget them. I still have no idea what it was that I saw on that one definitive night but I was more awake than ever, because of course I was stunned and confused why the lucid-dreaming had stopped in the first place, and I was still jarred; frightened; horrified of something I had seen, with no recollection of what it was. My body tensed and I kept my eyes closed…waiting. For what - I don't know. But my mind was never blank before in my entire life. There were always busy thoughts in my head – and now I also had curiosity, but I saw absolutely nothing. I hoped for an explanation but gave up on that rather quickly. Then I hoped for more symbols - but none came. The lucid-dreaming was indeed over. Something strange had interrupted my access to the subconscious. Something dark. Something terrifying.

The only thing in front of me was darkness; emptiness; still and distant. Then slowly an image emerged and it was like I had an aerial view looking down a long curved tunnel, and I could "feel" that from the bottom of this long, long tunnel there was an intense "hurting." *What did that mean?* Nothing like this had ever happened before. But, curious, I lay motionless, waiting for an explanation. I ached along with the heavy hurt emanating out of the long, curved, seemingly endless tunnel.

Then suddenly, from the corner of my closed eyes, a couple smears of light flew into the tunnel! Then a few more light bodies dove in at top speed, projecting so much love and concern that it gave me goose bumps. My empathetic aching was overridden by a feeling of exhilaration. I have no idea where those lights came from - I just saw those little beings dash past my eyes from both sides of my face, and downward toward the hurt. But the hurt at the tunnel bottom suddenly increased, and as it did, more dizzying flying smears of light flew in, along with their "love."

In another minute there were dozens and then hundreds of these lighted entities blurring past my eyes! The love they carried was pure and intense and relaxed my whole body! But the guttural pain in the tunnel still existed which I felt in my stomach.

In a few more seconds, thousands of tiny light bodies dove into this mysterious tunnel of pain. The entire view was flocked with these beings and that shocked me so much I threw open my eyes and I blurted, frightened, "Armageddon!" I was not religious but that word shot out of me.

I looked over at Doug who was sound asleep. I lay awake for hours, petting our sleeping Chihuahua, perplexed. What had just happened to me?! It wasn't a dream! I was fully awake!

In the morning Doug woke me to tell me to come downstairs to the living room and see the TV. A plane had crashed into the World Trade Center. By the time I got downstairs another plane had crashed into the other tower and we all know that the twin towers eventually imploded to the ground, killing thousands of people.

Wow.

I was shown the night prior that these thousands of people who were dying right now in front of me on TV were going to be met immediately by thousands of individual caring light smears (spirit guides?)!

Was this proof of life after death?

Was this proof they did not suffer long?

The tall towers resembled the curved long tunnel I saw, because I was seeing it from above.

What was I supposed to do with this message?

I told my friends and family and the waitresses at Canters deli, where I was then waiting tables – this was between my soap opera fame and artist career. They knew I wasn't the type to make-up stories so I know they believed me but wondered what horrible image it was that I needed to forget seeing. I don't think I'll ever know. Maybe someday I'll go under hypnosis to try to see it again.

I felt compelled to put this 9/11 premonition into my 2009 memoirs FORGIVING TROY but my friends convinced me that strangers would not believe me. So I kept it out. But time and time again I felt it deserved to be put back in, and editors convinced me to remove it because it would pull the focus off the story of my family. So I left it out.

But it nags at me.

Why did this happen?

Wasn't I intended to share it?

Since I was a little boy I have believed in spirit guides, or felt watched by invisible entities, all the while feeling protected by them. As I grew up I never felt alone, because, well, I never believed I was actually alone. I always believed there was a world around me, but one which I could not see.

Every day I have asked spirit guides that I have never seen, to be of assistance to me and particular friends needing help. Perhaps the reason I had this vision is because I have always been open to the idea of spirits, and life-after-death. And the fact that I had this vision the night before 9/11 is proof that I had not created this in my imagination. I experienced a premonition of the loving smears of light helping the thousands of dying people the night before the planes hit the towers.

Why?

Is it true that everything happens at once and while it appears as if I was receiving information about the future, I was actually experiencing it in real time adjusted for our Earth-Time continuum?

Many other people have had unexplainable occurrences involving what appears to be spirit guides coming to the rescue so I have compiled this book, a collaboration of accounts from credible sources, to help readers be inspired - and lifted out of their everyday worries.

We can so easily be depressed by bills we owe or romances that aren't working, or demands of work, or family, or society. We carry around stress and get distracted; sucked into a negative state of mind.

This collection of true-life spiritual accounts was compiled to remind us of the bigger picture.

We are not alone.

We are never alone.

"They" are there to protect us.

"They" are there to guide us.

"They" are there to help us.

"They" want to help us.

CHAPTER 2   WHY I COULDN'T FIND MY SPIRIT GUIDES THE WEEK OF 9/11

by Craig D.

All my life I felt presences. Being an electrical engineer, I thought it made complete sense for another dimension of electricity, like spirits, to exist, and having endured a childhood of challenges, I felt guarded, protected, comforted by these spirits. I have to tell you my story about "after 9/11" and how the guides explained it for me. I half-jokingly asked them "Was anyone home?", because I was feeling really alone for about a week and usually could feel a presence or two around my home. Basically, about 9/11, they told me, without the use of audible words, just words inside my head, that they knew something was coming, but that when it did it come was bigger and more devastating than they expected, so they (yes, they) were overwhelmed. Remember those stories that people working at ground-zero felt the presence of "invisible beings?" Well, my guide friends said there were many, many of those who died who did not know they were dead or what to do next, so the guides were having to try to help them cross over.

It sounds like a Bruce Willis movie, but I believe it was what happened: the walking dead. So many of those souls were taken so suddenly and with such brutal force that they were in limbo and needed help in completing their passage. Yes, the guides were somewhat busy and unavailable (or at least delayed in responding) to those of us here. They've told us that while they can see the future, their accuracy is NOT at 100% because every one of us here has free will and that makes everything somewhat "in-flux."

Many, many people are very curious about the spirit world but most of us are raised to reject it and stick with the old-time religion. Still, they have a hunger for this information and I think really want to believe. All it takes is hearing the right story from the right person and suddenly the world opens up for them! If one or 10 or 1 million people connect with spirit because of these accounts, we will have helped and healed, so let's do what the voices (the guides) tell us, and share this information. There is not right or wrong, just what IS.

Thom Bierdz: Between some chapters you'll see some of my spiritual paintings. This 9/11 piece is in my Tarot-like book, *THE BLUE X CARDS + 200 DIVINATION READINGS*. To see this in color, or get more info on my books, please go to www.ThomBierdz.com.

CHAPTER 3   SMELL OF DEATH FLOWERS: PLANE CRASH IN 1975

by Morris

Many individuals throughout their life have experienced unexplainable situations. Some that reoccur more than once in their life. They are realistic asking the question, "Why me?" Being reared in Virginia under the guidance of a Protestant father and mother, I was always told these types of situations happen for a reason, and that some individuals were gifted for having the foresight of an event about to happen and the event actually occurs. Today, I am still having the strange occurrence - the smell of DEATH - impending death of individuals. The smell of death that happens when particular flower odors occur. If you are familiar with the tiger lily plant family, you will have an idea of the odor that awakens me when this situation is present with me - generally always when I was asleep. Awakening to a strong odor in the middle of normal sleep. The odor that was affecting my breathing to the point that I must get out of the bed and stand up and try to take deep breaths. My bedroom was the general size room within most brick ranchers. Room for a single bed, dark brown desk and chair, and a brass desk lamp and a stereo phonograph. A wooden framed photograph of Jesus Christ was directly above my bed. My breathing was beyond my allergies-asthma problems. I noticed I was sweating somewhat. The odor I could not figure out was forcing me to feel the need for outside air. Moving through the house in total darkness to the back door seemed such a distance. Down into the laundry room where the backdoors were located and trying to find the electrical switch for the yard light. Before stepping out into the night air (28 degrees) I grabbed my corduroy coat and pushed my feet into my fur lined bedroom slippers. I realized something was really different as to what was happening to me. Cold like death in itself. Looking toward the deep night sky filled with stars, I began to take deep breaths again and then the feeling I was about to pass out. What was occurring was taking place for a reason - was it my time to die? For some reason, I could not move any further.

My mother must have awakened due to the cold air entering the house, as I forgot to close the door. She guided me back into the house, into the kitchen where my inhaler stayed, and forced me to taking a few sprays. She then handed me a wash cloth that had been rinsed with cold water for the forehead. She was in hopes that the cold water would assist in bringing my breathing and mental senses around. I could still smell the odor - the odor I could not explain! I remained the rest of that night sitting in a blue recliner, fighting the thought of how close was I to actual death.

Was this the actual odor that individuals had before death? If so, did I actually pass my own death, or was this God's way relating death was about to occur - but to whom? After a couple of hours sleep, I awakened looking out our den's large window that overlooked our backyard. There was no sunshine, a very cloudy day with wind blowing the large oak trees. All the grass was covered with frost and had a glistening appearance. With no appetite, I moved from the recliner, but felt absolutely weak throughout my body. The carpet felt so good to my bare feet, until I walked into the kitchens linoleum floor which was cold. Cold like death I thought. What happened, was something about to happen to someone in my family?

My parents came into the kitchen, and we discussed the issue of what occurred the previous night. I told my parents that it was totally different than anything I had experienced. I was still feeling like something horrible was about to happen, and I believed I experienced the sensation that people feel before physical death. They looked at me as though I just had a bad nightmare that created a breathing situation similar to asthma. But why was there an overpowering odor with this situation? What was this odor? I had to explain that the odor was still with me, but my breathing was better.

My parents were determined to change my thoughts for the day. They decided to take me with them to visit grandfather in the hospital, and go out to the shopping mall to look at some new trousers I was in need of. We never made it to the hospital. At 11:15AM my grandfather was dead. Although he was suffering from cancer, a cerebral hemorrhage struck and out of this world he passed. No more physical pain must my grandfather suffer. The odor that had started during the night with an unusual breathing problem was gone. THE ODER was GONE! I cried most of the day. I was breathing normally now and the odor was gone.

Mom really worried about me, as it was every time I told her about the odor. I cannot stand the calla scent and as to this very day, I have a phobia with those flowers. This has been with me before I ever went to a funeral home for anyone. In fact, the first time I realized this unusual sensation, I was only 16 - and the first one that died was my Sunday school teacher I truly thought so much about. He was only 42. He died from a cerebral hemorrhage.

He was a funeral director working at J. T. Morris. He had just waited on a family, returned to his desk to finish paper work, and said "I have a terrible headache." That was it. That was on a Tuesday. He was at church Sunday, and his typical self.

He was an interesting teacher. My parents were friends as they got together often and played cards. I told mom to get rid of the flowers in the house as it was disturbing my breathing. I had hay fever bad then. Mom said there were no flowers in the house. I told her I smelled flowers, but it was disturbing my breathing. She asked me what I was upset about. Oh well- you and I know the big issue I was dealing with.

A terrible tragedy occurred back in 1975, and many people were killed in an air disaster. I was visiting a married couple out in Merced, California, the day before I was to return home, that dead smelling odor struck me at breakfast. It was so bad, Thom, that I could not get my breath, and I became light headed. I could not get words out that made sense (Roy and Toni thought I was having a stroke).

They took me outside and sat me next to their pool - I do not remember leaving the kitchen and sitting next to the pool. One of their neighbors was a general practitioner, and he came over. I was very clammy and shaking. All I was saying - someone is going to die, someone is going to die and I do not know who. I made them all get away from me as I could not get my breath. It was like the flowers were all around me - from my feet - above my head. Every time I looked up towards the sky - the "LIGHT WAS SO BRIGHT" and this went on for over any hour… they all wanted me to go to the hospital. They said I was crying and all that was coming out of my mouth - "SOMEONE IS GOING TO DIE".

Those death flowers chase me - do you understand what I am telling you?! That doctor gave me something to relax me, but I was zonked out the rest of the afternoon. I awoke in the early part of the evening that day. The odor gone - but I had one extremely tired body.

Roy and Toni kept an eye on me the rest of the evening. The doctor left another pill to help me to sleep. Nevertheless, I was awakened during the night, and this time I had to throw up, sweating profusely - and again, the flowers were around me. The next morning, outside I went for air, then in an hour I flew out of SFO to JFK, and changed planes there to get back to Richmond.

Apparently, Roy and Toni had called my parents and told them what had happened and they were worried as they knew my death flowers incidents always resulted in fatalities. I was on a TWA 747 Jumbo from SFO to JFK. We left on time - had an hour and a half for my connection to Richmond. I was flying to Richmond on Eastern Air Lines. Half way through the TWA flight, this odor got a hold on me - I tried my air vent, and asked the lady sitting next to me if she could turn hers my way that I was having a breathing issue. I had to get up and move around.

The flight attendant saw I was having a breathing issue. I told her that I was smelling flowers so strong - was there any shipment of flowers aboard. She said no and took me to the upper deck lounge with some help. By then I was almost in tears and so embarrassed. I told her something bad very bad was going to happen.

The crew had no idea I was an experienced air traveler. They thought I was just overly concerned about the turbulence we had been encountering and expressed I was on one of the best aircraft built. I already knew that, but I could not get away from these flowers. She fixed me a Jack Daniels on the rocks.

In fact, the Captain, a tall slender gentleman, came out and spoke to me for a few minutes. He was full of compassion. I was honest with him, and told him what was happening. Of course, I told him "someone is going to die" and it would be soon. They had made plans to get me to the Eastern terminal as quickly as possible upon arrival at JFK. Well, the drink helped. I was just so worked up. The closer we got to New York, it seemed like that lounge was just full of death flowers. We encountered a severe electrical storm and circled for some time near New York.

We went into serve thunderstorm weather that soaked the entire North Eastern Atlantic Coast. The storm created a situation as where we were in a holding pattern between Ohio and Pennsylvania. Since the weight of the B747 is well over 400,000 lbs., she cannot just land at any airport. The flight I was on was to continue on to Milan, Italy after a 90 minute layover at JFK. Since the TWA and Eastern terminals were practically side by side, I should have no problem with my connection. But I was really suffering with that odor, but thank God the flight crew was just great.

The remaining few passengers that were in the upper deck lounge with me left when the Captain came out. Just me, the two flight attendants and the Captain. I told him why I was saying what I was saying. He felt with the weather not being good, that had a lot to do with me being nervous, but didn't believe death was imminent.

The stewardess fixed me another drink. I drank it down. I was able to stand, and the two attendants followed me down to the main floor and saw that I was seated. The turbulence became more. The captain made an announcement that if he did not receive permission within 30 minutes to land at JFK, the only other airport we could land at would be Montreal. Boston had closed as the storm front was just beginning there.

The lightning between the clouds was something else. The odor was so strong that I thought I was going to blackout, and the tears were in my eyes - I just knew death was around the corner. With the odor being so intense, I only had to consider this is the day that I will die. I kept thinking about my parents, and those I had just left in Calif.

The aircraft made a steep left banking procedure, and leveled off extremely quick. The captain asked us to tighten our seat belts as the landing may be a bit rocky and rough. As we finally came out of the clouds, a large body of water was below us. Did not know - but we flew right by the Statue of Liberty (sitting on right side). The aircraft engines became very loud and we started descending rapidly. My heart was now in my throat - I looked out the window and a very bright flash of lightning went off. Too close for comfort.

We started down over Jones Beach (Long Island) and the Queens major highway into JFK. To our shock, on the right side were the remains of a crashed aircraft. I knew it had to be very bad as there was so many fire trucks, police cars, ambulances on a much backed up highway. We dropped down to a runway no distance from this horrible sight - landing on a runway not even reinforced for the weight of the 747. The brakes were put to their ultimate test and luckily passed, but screeched at a deafening noise level. My face almost went into the seat in front of me. We came to a complete halt on this runway. You could have heard a pin drop it was so quiet in the cabin for a couple of minutes. The flight attendant that was with me came to me and asked "are you alright?"

Amazingly, the Death Flower odor was GONE!!!

I knew that the Death Angel had been with me, and I was going to witness something that horrible. The death odor CEASED when we passed the crashed aircraft. The down aircraft was an Eastern Air Lines B727 Jet. I was to transfer to Eastern, and the flight crew knew I was. When all was said and done, TWA took me personally over to Eastern in a ground vehicle to the jet way that my aircraft was located. There was only one runway open for takeoffs.

Many of the airlines were cancelling flights. Eastern was one, but also had a few departures. The Richmond flight was full (the last flight to Richmond from JFK for that day). The aircraft that I returned home on was also a Boeing 727 Jet. Exactly like the crashed one. I was so numb, and sick to my stomach, I was asked if I would like to go to medical department at JFK. I just sat- with nothing to say.

We boarded. The flight crew on the Eastern flight was told about me, and they looked after me. Once we arrived to the long line of planes waiting their turn to take off, we were facing a field of red and blue flashing lights. Morgue vehicles crossing taxiways.

The captain asked that everyone sitting on the right side, (which I was on), please pull down the window shades. We were informed that lightning had struck that aircraft. The internet has the details on crash of Eastern Flight 66.

That June 24th was a day I will never forget. The crash and the odor - those death flowers could have been meant for me as well. I felt I was about exhausted of any oxygen. Could there have been possibly - "a death ANGEL" sitting with me? I was supposed to be back in Richmond at 8:30 PM. I arrived back in Richmond at 12:55 AM.

My friends back in California were very stunned when they heard of the air crash. They called the house at 2:15 AM - 11:15 M PDT.

They just kept saying - my God, we could not believe it. I told them the flower odor was gone, but not until we passed the wreckage. That event of death flowers took the strength out of me for a couple of days. I saw my doctor who then decided I needed to see a specialist in this field. My parents thought a local "head doctor" could be just as valuable to explain these questionable odors.

Was a few years before I boarded a plane and returned to California for a visit.

I took care of my parents through their illnesses, and went to the retirement center to check on my father (dementia) practically every night. He would only allow me to help ready him for bed. To watch both of the ones I loved so much slowly die - there were no death flower odors. I was grateful for that. I have been keeping a close eye on my dad's twin sister. She lost her only child (33yrs old) on Christmas Eve of 1990. She was not married. She lost her husband in 1998 of Cancer - there was the odor of funeral callas (off and on) for ONE WEEK. Again, when it had moved into the strong mode, his death occurred within 24 hours.

Do not send me any callas, Thom.

CHAPTER 4   CHEROKEE'S CHRISTMAS MESSAGE FROM SISTER

by Don (also known as) Spirit Walker

I am a 65 year-old male of Native American descent, I was gifted at a young age of being able to prophecy and see things others could not. My mother had the same gift. I sometimes talk to the animals for I can know what they are thinking even though they never speak.

I guess you would say I am a traditionalist, I believe in the Great Spirit, and the teachings of the ancestors, as to the stories of Creation, too many to mention here. I believe we are all brothers under the skin, as do a lot of the Native People.

I was born in the autumn of 1954, I had a twin brother who died at birth, (lived 3 days; had a heart deformity), if that was today he would have survived. I also have a sister that was still born 11 months before me and my brother were born. I have 2 older sisters and 6 younger than I, 4 male, 2 female siblings. Which made a total of 11 children, through our raising, I basically was the only one of all the siblings who would listen to my mother when she would speak, and would try to learn of the ways of the people. It was not until I started attending Native Gatherings that I was told I had the gift of walking between both worlds, the world of the living, and the world of the spirits, and thus was given the name Spirit Walker.

I knew at a young age that I was able to do certain things, as was my mother. I could talk to people who had passed and give messages to the ones that they were intended for. My mother knew this and even though she would encourage me to do it, she would also discourage me, for fear of peer pressure, and people's anger toward others who are unusual and special.

It was not until 1988 after mom passed away that I decided to start learning about my heritage, not just Cherokee, but, all the nations that I could. I had the indescribable urge to learn all I could from them. So I would pray I proceeded to take my children and try to bring them up with the values that my mother had instilled in me, (with a lot of objection from my first wife), but, right after my Mother passed in 1988, I would pray as to why I was left and orphaned, (my dad had passed away when I was 3, and my stepfather had passed away when I was 28).

This went on for many years, I would read books of the Native Americans, watch any TV shows I could find - whatever it took to learn of them. Then I got wind of the Gatherings that they would have called powwows, so I started attending them, as often as I could, and I listened to the story tellers tell of the ancient ways of the people, and how they would worship, and how they loved mother earth, and all things.

One night in 1994 I was I guess in a dream state when in my bedroom appeared to me (now mind you I thought I was dreaming this, but, it was so real) 4 Native American Men, They called themselves the 4 Elders of the Sacred Fire. One of them stepped forward, he called himself Walking Stick, he was donned in all buffalo attire and carried a rattle, and had a buffalo headdress atop his head. He said to me "We come for you, you have a lot to learn my son."

Instantly I was taken to a place, not sure where, it looked like the old west with the bare ground, and Native Tepees in the background, I was placed in front of a raging fire, and I could see all the colors of the flames, the red, yellows and oranges.

But, I thought it was strange that I felt no heat from the fire. Walking Stick proceeded to speak, "You have been brought here, my son, to know of your journey, down the Red Path of life, (I call it the red road). We are the Spirit guides that have been chosen to assist you on your journey. I am Walking Stick, this is Walks A Lot (he looked extremely old and used a walking stick to get around). That is Black Elk, (well, we all know that Black Elk was a great Oglala Sioux holy man) and the last one is 3 Feathers On A Horse. This was a younger man(younger than the others), had a shaved head, what looked like war paint on half his face and he was on the largest horse I have ever seen. Walking Stick proceeded to say, "The Great Spirit has work for you to do, my friend. It will be his work. He will bring those in need to you, and you, with our teachings, will lead them to the Red Road, to follow the path of the ancestors."

The next thing I remember was waking up in the bed, drenched in sweat, and wondering if it was real. Well, I find out that it is real, and I realize that I am beginning to learn more and more and I am able to do things after this that I have not done before.

These 4 Elders have been a major part of my life whenever I have done any readings for anyone or they have brought anyone to me that is in need of guidance. I have been asked by many, "Why are you not charging money for this ability?" but, honestly, I cannot ask a price for something that was given to me as a gift. I just ask for friendship and kindness to be my payment as that is what the Great Spirits teaches us.

I would like to give you an experience I have had and it took place Christmas Day, 2007.

Pam, my eldest sister (eldest of 11 children) passed away on August 22, 2006, after finding out 11 days before that she had Leukemia.

My sister has just retired from being a Nursing Assistant for 37.5 years in June of 2006; she had 2 grown children and 4 grandchildren. She had turned 60, in June of 2006 and passed in August, she was only able to enjoy her retirement for about 8 weeks, and had only gotten her first Social Security check. Pam was the mediator for the rest, she kept the trouble at bay, when one of the siblings had a problem with the other one, and she made it a point to as she would say, "NIP IT IN THE BUD."

Pam took over the role as mother when mom passed in 1988, for some of the siblings depended on our mother it seemed like to breathe. But, Pam also did this for her children also, kept them close to her and Pam always did without so they could have.

But, she liked her beer, did not smoke, but, in her younger days she would be able to drink the best of them under the table. She was ornery and stubborn as a mule, but she was my sister and I loved her dearly.

I also have a sister Barb, who is also a Nursing Assistant, and Pam and her were like stuck at the hip, when she would come to visit.

I have a brother Dale, who is a wizard at fixing automobiles, this he does for a living. Brother Wayne drives a big rig for a local grain company. Brother Ike drives a front end loader for a trash company in Indiana.

Sister Virginia lives in Kentucky and over the years we have lost touch, but, Pam made it a point to keep in touch with all of us.

Baby brother Daniel lives in Cincinnati and works at a loan company as a loan officer.

This is a large group of siblings, but, over the years we have all went our own way, and usually only see each other at funerals when a family member passes. This is such a waste, but, sometimes people put material things before all that is important.

Me: I am a factory worker, have been most of my life, when to college when I was younger, wanted to make a difference, got an associate's degree in Mental Retardation, working with Downs Syndrome individuals, which I still do on occasion.

I have been married twice, the second wife is my soul mate, she now works at a Residence Home for the Disabled/Mentally Challenged, and loves it, and she has done this for many years. I myself was blessed with 2 beautiful children.

There were still 9 living when Pam, passed so now we are down to eight. It was devastation for all of us.

No one could figure out why this happened and I had ask the Great Spirit, and my own spirit guides (they call themselves the 4 Elders Of The Sacred fire) why I could not reach my sister, which I was able to do this for so many others. By that I mean I have been at a friend's house before when I mentioned that someone had passed in the house and that their spirit still remained there.

Many moons ago I walked into a house when my sister Pam and Ron were looking to rent, and I told them of the death in that house and how it took place and where it happened. They checked it out with the landlord and he had not told anyone for fear that it could not be rented. The spirit in that house was not into company or anyone else living there. I had a brother-in-law that passed in 1996, and I was told in the hospital to go and pray. When I did the 4 Elders Of The Sacred Fire appeared to me and in detail told me of the impending death of my brother-in-law and what steps had to be taken that night to make sure everyone could see him before he passes.

I also do have the gift of seeing the Death Angel before someone passes, not the one that is shown in the Dickens classic, or in cartoons or sci-fi. This is a beautiful golden stream of light with a halo at the top and what looks like soft white wings at the side, and I can see its hand outstretched, engulfing the person that is going to pass. I have seen this at least 8 times in the last 10 years.

The night Pam passed I walked into the room (she was in a hospital about 100 miles from where I live), and the doctor informed me that they were going to take the life support off her. I looked at him and casually said, "She is already gone, for I saw her leaving with the Death Angel, and this is her shell. Her spirit has returned home." He looked at me like I was 4 different colors, and sent the resident psychotherapist to talk to me. And again I told them what I saw, they shrugged it off like I was in shock, let them think what they want, I know what I saw.

These are the kinds of things that I experience each day. 3 weeks before Bob Hope died I saw his death, and the death of the Pope John Paul II, and I have seen the spirits of the ones from 9/11 and helped some cross over. If anyone ever watched the *Ghost Whisperer*, some of the things that were on that show can and do actually happen.

When I would team up with a Native American woman that I am great friends with, I would teach a class on the culture of the people and the ways of the ancestors.

But I could not contact Pam's spirit. To this I prayed and meditated, and I kept doing my readings for others and tried assisting them as I have done before. But that particular night - Christmas - I had been praying more.

I pray anywhere the notion strikes me but my sacred spot is in my bedroom by the side of my bed with my native beads. I pray to the Great Spirit the last thing at night, and pray the first thing when I awaken. I will pray at work, in my car, at my computer when I am reading an email, and am not sure what the spirits want me to say I pray for guidance and knowledge to be able to assist this person (whomever it may be) on their life's journey.

Granted I pray a lot and the answers do not come instantly as many people think they should, for the Great Spirit works in HIS time, and in his way. We may think this is the best for us, but, he will answer the prayer in another fashion, to show us, that another way was even better.

I am a firm believer that you can pray anywhere, but, when you want to get to the nitty-gritty, go to your sacred spot.

So – finally I got visited by my sister.

She said, "Hello Goob," and when she manifested to me it was not the Pam that had left a year ago - it was the sister from many years back that looked younger and more vibrant than she had in years.

Let's just say that Christmas is full of miracles. She said, "Thought I would drop in on you since you have been praying for me. Well, I am fine and I have lost so much weight, Donnie I am not sure how they do it here but I look 30 years younger."

Thom, or Little Hawk as I see you, I have explained to you I hope what you have asked for and it is from my heart, that I say WADO to you for letting me be a part of your book.

Pam, from the afterlife, said "Mighty fine, mighty fine, I see that Mary is still working as hard as ever, she is a good woman, and a hard worker - give her my love. Tell her I think it is honorable what you guys are doing for David, as he had no other place to go and the creeps that he was living with was using him.

"Sorry to hear about Deanna and Eddie, and Bill and Annie getting a divorce. The guy that Deanna is seeing now looks like a nice guy. He seems ok; I have popped in on her once and a while. Hell, she doesn't even know I am there.

"Mom is here and man, she looks good, as does Betty. We all look so young, and our dad is here and Donnie, guess what, he has hair! I had never seen him with hair.

"I have watched Tiffany work herself up into a tizzy, and for the life of me cannot believe why. She was always more like the Smith's than my side. David just rolls with the flow.

"I know you talked to Ronnie, tell him that I love him and there will be a place for him when it is his time. Max will be here with me before long, so tell him to be prepared for that. But, let him know that he will be well of any sickness that he has.

"Donnie, You and Barb keep in contact with him for he thought a lot of you guys.

"I see that Barbara and Kenny are back together, she needs to know that I am glad for her.

"She needs to know that the way she is feeling is dumb and I am a lot safer here then I was there. I am free of any illnesses or pain. I do not have to have a heart monitor, like I did, and there is no stress over here. Just sit around and gossip all day.

"Norma is here with me now and is telling me to tell Mary that she never meant for her to be taking care of David, at this point in her life. Norma thought he would have already been gone after Scott passed. She wants to say thank you for all you have done for David and she really loves you, she says you should have known that but, she will say it anyway.

"Tell Tonya and Dave I said howdy, and that I have talked to some of her kin over here also.

"I have been watching over Chris. You and Mary should be proud of him, for being able to do on his own, so far away.

"Well, little brother, I going to get going and wanted to say Merry Christmas to you and Barb and Tonya and Mary and Ronnie, and everybody else.

"Be good. Bicycle. Love you all! Pam."

Now that was the message that I got! She always called me Goober, as it fascinated her on the gift that I had to communicate with people who passed. She always ended a conversation with Bicycle instead of Bye or Good-bye. She always thought that Good-bye would be forever and Bicycle meant you kept on rolling with it.

CHAPTER 5   A TENNIS PRO'S DEATH AND MIRACULOUS RETURN

by Jim K.

Working as a professional line official in professional tennis events is stressful enough.

On July 3, 2003 I started work at an event in Orange County, California. Since I live in the Los Angeles area, it's a big commute. Another umpire and I decided to carpool for the four days we would be at this event. He drove that first day, picked me up very early. We hit Starbucks and then drove down to the site of the event.

It was long and hot and as the day progressed, I became more and more nauseous, listless, and totally uninspired to do anything. This was not my usual style. I was quite a diligent tennis professional. Later in the day I could hardly function and it was all I could do to keep myself from sitting or lying down somewhere in the grass. As the organizers of this event knew me and my record, they had concerns and sent the event trainer to have a look at me. She took my blood pressure, temperature, things they could do at an event and she advised me that if I did not feel better the next day, I should schedule an appointment with my doctor.

The balance of the day continued the same for me and finally we were able to leave and go home. The drive home was extremely long and I was nauseous beyond belief. I finally arrived home and decided I did not want to eat but took a shower and decided to have a glass of wine to try to settle my stomach and watch some TiVo. It was already well into the evening and that is my last recollection of events until much later the following day.

The next day I was to be the driver and pick my umpire friend up on the way to the event in Orange County. True to form, I apparently got up, showered, dressed in the tournament clothing, and headed out to my sports car to pick up my friend. My route from my house includes many small side streets, hills, etc.. Having driven a few blocks and crossed the main street of San Vicente Boulevard, I proceeded through the intersection and started a downhill descent on a narrow street with many parked cars and apartment buildings and homes along the way. Again, none of this is any memory to me.

At some point, I lost consciousness and somehow turned off the street directly into the side drive of the West Hollywood Fire Department and crashed into their building, as opposed to parked cars or some other structure - one of a string of many miracles to happen to me very early that July 4th morning. The crash apparently was noisy enough to awake some of the firemen who found me and my crashed car in their drive. I was clinically dead at the scene with no heartbeat. Because of where I was and the training for the firemen, they were able to restart my heart and transport me to nearby Cedars Sinai Medical Center within the few minutes they had to revive and stabilize me. More reasons to love firemen.

Not recalling any of this because, as I was later told by many doctors, my body was already going into shock the day before because my heart was shutting down. I was rushed to the emergency room amid a great deal of commotion for emergency surgery to clear a blockage and stabilize my condition. I was placed in a bed in ICU along with my officials bag I always carried which included the necessities, wallet, phone, sun block and eye cream. At some point while still unconscious, I apparently located my cell phone and with only one contact lens still intact, was able to phone the people most important in my life - some very close friends and special people.

I regained consciousness early evening to find myself somewhere I had no idea of and facing all of the special people in my life who were in the area. They had all received my message in which I told them I had a bad accident and was in Cedars ICU and could they come and help me. They all did. How I made those phone calls or even knew where I was is a mystery as I still have no recollection of those events although a subsequent visit to the operating room during my stay at Cedars brought flashbacks of commotion, fright, and faces who attempted to be kind to me in my out of control state.

I immediately told them the story of having had an accident and crashing my car, walking the few blocks back home, deciding I was injured and walking to Cedars emergency, deciding the emergency room was too hectic and I wanted nothing to do with it, walking back home and deciding I was indeed injured and returning to the emergency room where they admitted me to the hospital. They basically said, "What the heck?"

Support, love, priorities and miracles are what this story is about. When you are seriously down, there is nothing more important than a true friend, faith, and the ability to learn from situations and give that back to those you really connect with.

I was subsequently released from the hospital a week or so later and returned home for a recovery period. That first evening alone was scary. There was still a good amount of pain from surgeries and the realization that I had been given a special gift in my life had not fully settled in. My recollections are sketchy as to the many acquaintances and co-workers who stopped by the hospital to visit and for a long time I heard from people who had visited me or spoken to me on the phone that I had no recollection of. So at that point I was pretty unsettled.

My first morning back home began with coffee at a local spot and sitting outside and reading the newspaper. It was fantastic. Returning home, I was still unsettled about what happened to me and being as independent as I am, I decided to test myself and headed out on a long walk very uphill to Sunset Boulevard because I just needed to know I was not going to drop over somewhere. It was a silly idea but I made it up those hills and even though I had to call a friend to pick me up and drive me home and endure a lecture about recovery from a medical person, I felt I had accomplished something for myself.

Call it denial but I was back on a professional tennis court three weeks later and worked events through major professional sports events the remainder of that summer. This was not well received when I reported back to my cardiologist. Looking back now I see a lot of silliness and unwillingness to accept my situation in all of that. A subsequent visit at the West Hollywood Fire Department, and time with the special people in my life, have given me the realization of what really matters in life and priorities of the special people in your life as opposed to self-satisfying adventures.

Remembering only flashes of that day and the contacting of my special group is a serious blessing. Their reaction to the situation speaks highly of them and the great fortune I have in finding these people over many years of experiences and staying with them. Now we are even more of a part of each other's lives.

My event was on the news. It had higher odds than of winning the lottery. Something outside my conscious self orchestrated events to get me help from firemen to a hospital which saved my life.

CHAPTER 6   HOW DO I TELL ACEY WHEN HE WILL DIE?

by Steve S.

I moved from AZ to LA to work as an actor. After some success on stage and a gig as a tour guide at Universal Studios, I found myself back in retail. In October of 1994, I was once again unemployed, taking screenwriting classes and working on a book in my spare time. Six months earlier had I quit my job as a retail clerk at Bullock's department store in The Beverly Center feeling lost and confused. My heart just wasn't in retail. I wanted something meaningful to do. Daniel, a friend from Bullock's, called and told me he'd left Bullock's not long after I did and was happily working now in an antique store in Beverly Hills. He invited me to dinner to catch up and meet his new boss Acey. I said Sure! Where? He told me: West Hollywood at a place called 'Figs' a popular hangout on Santa Monica Blvd. I thought great, it's not far from my apartment, I can actually walk.

Daniel was concerned that Acey liked him a bit too much and wanted me to act as a safe third wheel at dinner. When I asked him if he felt the same way about Acey, he said No, Acey has AIDS. I thought, *wow, Daniel's harsh. Acey's a human being, isn't he*? But then I thought, if this Acey liked me, I'd probably be afraid of getting intimate with him, too. It was 1994, men were dying right and left and the panic AIDS created was huge. A good friend of mine had died of AIDS six years earlier in AZ. He never told anyone he was sick. I called him before Christmas 1988 to see him and was told by an angry coworker of his that he'd died several months earlier. I was devastated. We were so close, I thought. *Couldn't he trust me?* I realized the shame he felt must have been unbearable to live with in addition to all of the physical symptoms he was dealing with.

I looked forward to meeting Acey. When I did, I thought what a cute spin on a Clark Kent type! Gold wireframe glasses, six feet tall, slightly muscular though slim, impish Irish grin, with brownish-blonde hair and crystal blue eyes. His personality was sunny and wild yet calming and introspective. He could be the life of the party and still be the quiet poet in the corner. He was wonderful. His smile was so bright. Yet the underlying fatigue seemed to wear on him. He wasn't eating much of his dinner at all. I could sense he was trying as hard as he could to be 'up' for this evening and yet his body seemed to be fighting him on it. He leaned heavily on the table for support and rose up slowly when he went to the restroom a couple times during our dinner. I appreciated his valiant effort and I felt so terribly bad that he was sick. It broke my heart. I wanted to take all his sickness away and give him his health back. I silently wished that I could take it on. Throughout the dinner I became slowly weaker and weaker, feeling as if I needed a major rest and a vacation. I lost my appetite completely. It's like we had exchanged bodies.

Not knowing why this was happening, I did manage to stay until dinner was over and at the end of the evening I went home and right to bed. I slept for hours. The next day I was still feeling beat. (I discovered years later that I have strong empathic abilities.)

Always knowing since I was young that I have incredible inner strength, I had asked God for Acey's pain and suffering that night out of my sorrow for him, not realizing it was actually possible to get it! (They say watch what you ask for. You may get it!) And with deep sorrow about his health and condition, and genuine interest in helping him, I actually took on his sickness and gave him my life force. (Not recommended for anyone to try this).

He ended up having a great dinner that night. Laughing loudly, getting stronger and stronger with every passing minute, he even commented he never felt this strong. It was as if he was 100% healed. Even with the discomfort and physical price I paid, I'm glad I was able to give him that evening of health.

I stayed in touch with Daniel and saw Acey several times after that at Daniel's house. They had become good friends. And I was happy to see Acey smile and laugh (quietly) on a regular basis. I never asked for his pain and suffering again and therefore was able to hold my own energy whenever I saw him.

Daniel asked if I'd go with him to Acey's home for Thanksgiving in 1994. I said sure! The night before, while in bed waiting to fall asleep, I had a vision. I was awake with my eyes closed and I saw Acey die. He was in bed and simply lifted up out of his body. I felt this euphoric joy that I can't even begin to describe. I felt LOVE so intense and so beautiful that my description of it doesn't even come close to the intensity and deepness of this Joy and Love. It was amazing! Like nothing I'd ever experienced on Earth. Acey was lifted out of his body racked with pain and agony and he was suddenly a new man. Happy, vital, and filled with this amazing LOVE and PEACE. When it was over, I opened my eyes and suddenly worried. *Oh NO! Does this mean he just died? He'll be dead tomorrow when we get there?* Luckily no. He was very much alive the next day.

His house was decorated in antique early American. His parents (two charming, easy-going people from the Midwest) had helped him with the floral centerpiece and both of them made me laugh with their jokes and folksy humor. Everything tasted incredible. His mom sure knew how to use spices.

Throughout the day I felt a deep nagging to tell him about my vision of him from the night before. But I ignored it. HOW could I tell him he was going to die? We were all hoping for a cure. This was two years before the cocktail of antivirals came out.

After enough of the persistent nagging, I gave in. I knew he needed this information, and I was supposed to give it to him. So, I had a moment in the kitchen alone with him and I told him I wasn't sure how to tell him this but...and I told him everything. He stood enraptured listening to every word. He thanked me for telling him. He said it gave him incredible peace. He'd been worried about death and dying. It scared him immensely even the thought of it - since he'd never known anyone that had ever died. He was 35 years old and still had both sets of grandparents. He did say that recently a girl he knew only slightly from high school had visited him in a dream and told him she would be guiding him over. Though he really never knew her that well, she said she would help him transition. He woke up assuming she must be dead.

Acey died seven months later. It was sad to hear he was gone. Though I knew he was loved, happy, joyous, peaceful and healthy INSTANTLY! I was happy I trusted that instinct to tell him about my vision. It definitely made a difference in his last months here on planet Earth. And really set him at ease.

I would have never guessed that in meeting Acey and getting to know him, I'd finally find closure in the relationship with my friend from AZ that I never had the chance to complete.

A year later I became a volunteer with AIDS Project Los Angeles, through Project Night Lite and assisted and eased those in hospitals and hospice care (whose families and friends had turned their backs on them) in their final days and hours as they were dying. Singing, holding their hands, sometimes just listening and being there for them as they crossed over so that no one would have to die alone. I feel blessed to have been a part of this amazing organization.

*And to help those who really needed it. How amazing life, is when we serve others and inadvertently ourselves!

CHAPTER 7   MY ONGOING RELATIONSHIP WITH THE DEAD

by Irene M. Galasso

My mother was of the first set of triplets ever born in the small Ukrainian village (Pykulovychi) in the year 1922. The excited priest named the three girls "Vera", "Nadia" and "Luba", in which, in the Old Ukrainian Language translated to Faith, Hope and Charity in English. When World War 2 Nazi bombs were hitting nearby, my mother, Vera (Faith) made her escape to Germany. There, she married a shoemaker and had children.

Baby Irene and mother Vera.

I, the eldest, was born in occupied West Germany (Bremerhaven) in the year 1946, with the priest given name *Helena*. I learned Ukrainian as my first and native language, although I attended a German school and spoke German as a child, while living in Germany. In the dawn of the American Industrial Age, when starving foreigners were being offered free transport on a ship to America, the American troops did everything they could to persuade my mother to leave Germany. She, dad, my two younger brothers and I, who was only five years old at the time, were documented immigrants traveling to Ellis Island.

Once in America, with only our clothes on our backs, we all crowded a cot above a saloon in Newark, New Jersey until we could afford to own a real home of our own. From there we eventually moved and purchased a rather spooky house on Montgomery Avenue in Newark, New Jersey from the previous residents who were a German family.

The basement of our new home scared the heck out of me, so I avoided it at all costs. Many were uncomfortable with that house's energy – I remember the plumber freaking out hearing footsteps above his head somewhere. There was one incident where suddenly my hands felt like they were on fire for a few minutes! Scorching heat!

When I was about ten years old, I was shocked to hear that my seven-year-old cousin, Sophia, had died at an emergency hospital due to a sudden illness, that I then could not even pronounce. Attending her wake and seeing her in the casket, she looked so very beautiful and alive. Many wonderful memories of her raced through my mind.

Sophia's grave.

Almost every night after her funeral I had nightmares - kept seeing her in her backyard in a white dress crying in the rain. Several sleepless nights later I finally told my mom about my dream, and then asked her – "Why is Sophia crying in the rain outside?" Mother assured me Sophia was certainly not in the rain outside, but about a week later after my persisting, she called Sophia's mother to tell her about my haunting nightmare… Her mother had then confided that elements of Sophia's death were hushed. Only a few adults had known the truth.

Sophia's mother had been entertaining a man, and locked Sophia outside. It was not raining at that point. Apparently, her mom was preoccupied and did not hear or bother to let Sophia in when it started to rain. When she did eventually answer the banging on the back door, she discovered her little daughter in dire pain, and rushed the shivering wet girl to the hospital, where they discovered her appendix had burst. It was too late. When my mother had finally told me the truth of what happened, the nightmares stopped. Perhaps Sophia wanted someone to know the truth of what really happened?

About that same time, in fourth grade, at recess I used to tell my friend Stephanie about my dreams and how I thought that something was wrong with my mind because I said, "I just don't believe Mom's husband is my real father." I would have dreams about a father figure, who looked, sounded and seemed different than the man I knew to be my father. Upon graduating high school, so many years later, I was working as a line lady at the phone company. A coworker next to me recognized my name and said, "My mom knows your mom. Did you know that the man your mom married is not your real father?" I said "okay," a bit confused, still I brushed it off. Later that day I decided to call my mom and ask her about my father, and she confirmed. I never knew my real father and somehow instinctively knew my step-father was not my biological father even though I had always been told otherwise.

My step-father was a great guy – usually – but when he got drunk, he sometimes lost his temper with Mom, sometimes he would even hit her. Rumor was he drank because of a tortured memory of his first wife, who he insisted they buried alive while pregnant (premature burials would sometimes happen back then). Apparently, one dark night as Dad maneuvered taverns, he felt compelled to approach a woman cloaked in black that he saw standing at the end of the road. He swears it was the spirit of his dead first wife, insisting he stop drinking and hurting Mom.

Another night, when I was 18, Dad was drunk. I came home and Mom seemed fearful of him. She asked me to lay with her on her bed. For no reason known to me, laying with Mom on the bed, I saw kaleidoscope-like images and became very over-protective of her. Almost as if I was possessed (by something, or even someone), I marched to the living room, throwing my step-father against the wall and saying he better never hurt mom again. Mind you, I was about 105lb. at the time, and yet, still, somehow threw a 6'1" 200lb. man against the wall. Never before this night and never again after did I act that way. It was like I was a different person for a few minutes.

Another time a dark shadow figure floated in my bedroom. It was a male. I was not threatened and actually could hear my little brother, John, and my father in the other room - so I could have screamed, and they would have come in if I was frightened. Even though this ghost-like entity would have scared others, it did not disturb me - and I just turned over and went to sleep. Occasionally throughout the years I did feel a presence next to me when I slept. In fact, I was so used to an entity in bed with me that when I felt my space was too invaded, I would try to push it back and off the bed. I did not share these strange experiences with anyone but many years later my younger brother, John's future wife, Eleanor, said that that house was haunted, and I would have to agree.

House on Montgomery.

When I was 19, I got engaged to my "first love" - Tony Mancuso. We had an epic year-long romance. It was very passionate, and he would always say to me, "He will never leave me." We were very much in love. One night, I was dreaming and suddenly a vision of Tony woke me up and I heard him clearly calling my name. He pleaded, "Irene. Hold my hand. Don't let go. Irene!! Hold on! Don't let go of my hand!" As if he was there with me, I felt him clutching onto my fingers, but slowly slipping away.

The next day (this was around the year of 1965) I found out that he had been murdered behind the Royal Theatre, in Bloomfield, NJ - he was shot in the head. He used to hang with a very questionable crowd. After his death I used to smell his Canoe cologne around my staircase. One week I saw flashes of Tony's death in my dream and said to my friends, "I saw Tony being put in the black car - he was not killed in the car like the police report said." I somehow knew that Tony knew the killers and they did not mean to kill him - they meant to kill someone else, but Tony got shot - "gangland style." I think Tony was framed for something he didn't really do and was mistakenly killed for it. I will never forget the feeling of being in his head and seeing his murder or him holding my hand... and him slipping away. I was later told when they shot him in the head he did not die instantly - he was awake a while, so I assume it was during that minute of struggling that he was reaching to me for help, trying to stay on the Earth plane - but he could not.

When I was around the age of 20, I was driving with my friend in my prized, yellow, 1964 Pontiac Catalina convertible (I felt so cool in that car), and the cops ended up pulling me over for no reason – I think they were trying to hit on us - we were attractive, young girls. I argued with them, probably pent up emotion on my part as I was still grieving over Tony, and the cops ended up throwing me into jail. Hours later when I was being bailed out, a detective named Dennis said, "I can't figure it out. The two cops that brought you in here – one got into an accident and the other one got beat up. You sure you didn't have something to do with it?!" I said no, but always had a feeling I was being protected by a higher source, or force.

For instance, another time I was at an intersection waiting for the light to turn green and something says to me, "Don't go." Totally weirded out, I just looked around – and seeing no one – stalled more, taking this in. A good thing, too, because in a second a car sped through the red light and would have killed me had I inched the car forward.

When I was 23, I met a man named Carman, we had a child, but I ended up leaving him when I found out he cheated on me with a woman named Mary. A few years later, my best friend Maryanne who I met at the line job decided to introduce me to her younger brother Robert – I knew he was the man I had visions of, as a child, when I lived in the house on Montgomery Avenue. I ended up running off and marrying this man in less than two weeks (his sister Maryanne dared us to get married and neither of us wanted to back out of the dare). I became the mother to his two children he had before me, and we ended up having two children of our own.

Other small psychic stuff happened in the next few years, like I knew what the sex of my babies were before I was told (I thought that was normal, and that I was supposed to know these things). Over the years I remembered that as a child the house on Montgomery Avenue had given me visions of birthing a daughter (I did not end up having her until the age of 38, which was 8 years after I had my first son with Robert). I named her Natalie – the Americanized version of my Moms triplet sisters name "Nadia"/ Hope.

Every time when I walked passed my co-worker named Andrea, I used to get this hot feeling - I got sweaty and my stomach was in knots - and I heard "ten million" in my head. This never happened elsewhere. I did not understand but assumed maybe I was going to win ten million dollars in the lotto. This seemed to be reassured every day and I started to spend the money in my mind, even promising the nuns at the church that when I win, I'll give them a percentage. That feeling was very strong the day I drove to Andrea's cousin's house to pick up merchandise for the upcoming Chinese auction at the church.

Guess who won ten million dollars two weeks later? Andrea's cousin! It was in all the papers!

When my Mom got cancer, I often slept next to her trying to soothe her pain and keep her optimistic. One night I woke from my sleep and turned around and there was a lady with blond hair standing next to the bed. Half-awake, I say "Go back to bed," (I thought it was my Mom trying to get out of bed). She was coming towards me and trying to hug me – I think, but I pushed her away. Later I realized it was not a real human but a spirit. Maybe it was her mother (my grandmother)? Three days later my Mom passed away.

I worked at a construction company office on the second floor of a three-story building. Above us lived 80-year-old woman named "Flo," who, at her age was still smoking like a chimney. She was a dear old broad and I would hang out and smoke with her on my lunch breaks. One day, something told me to say, "Flo, you should leave your door open because if anything happens to you, no one can get in. Leave the door open."

Two weeks later, one Sunday evening, everything is bothering me - my head - my stomach – and I felt I needed to see Flo. I asked my husband and teenage daughter to go, but they had other priorities, suggesting I wait a day and see Flo when I go to the office on Monday. "No, I need to go now," I insisted, and got in my station wagon and drove to her. I ran up the stairs and heard the old woman whimpering in her hoarse smoker voice.

Flo had fallen in her kitchen and could not get up. Unfortunately, I was not muscular enough to lift her, but I managed to pull her to the bedroom, and somehow got her onto the bed. I gave her juice and cake and left after she assured me she'd be fine. The next day she was, but I told my co-worker Sandy to alert her family to watch over her closely. Her cousin helped and arranged to put her in a nursing home.

A few weeks go by and on a Thursday, I heard a low voice, that was very clear, wake me up, "Irene. Ireeeeeeene." I rolled over to my husband and asked him, "What?" But he was sleeping and later insisted he did not call me. It happened again. I asked him – but he denied it was him.

Who was it? Well, the next day at work I was informed Flo passed away at 4 AM – exactly the time the low voice called my name. Initially I assumed it was a male voice, because my husband was the only one in the house with me, but it was her real voice, before it was affected by smoking and became hoarse. Feeling such a bond, I made sure to give Flo's bedroom set to my daughter, as Flo had asked me to do long ago. To this day, Natalie still has the bedroom set, over two decades later.

This daughter, Natalie, seems charmed by spirits as well – protected – benefited. Her sensitive energy always senses random things in the dark so she sleeps with her lights on even as an adult. If and when she gets in fights with people, weird stuff happens to them – they may trip and fall - some have even gotten carjacked, etc., as if she has spirit bodyguards. And she has the best luck! Every time she comes to my company party, she wins the big prize if she likes it – a TV – trip – you name it. My co-workers don't want her coming because she takes all the prizes. Or should I say spirits give her the prizes?

In later years, I had taken care of another sick woman, Mrs. Seizen – my boss's mother. I did this in my spare time to help since she lived right next door to my work building – this was not an official job - but she needed me, and I always made myself available. Every time I took her somewhere - the beauty parlor - or shopping - or did something for her, she'd insist on handing me $10. I didn't feel it was necessary but took it because she demanded I give it to my daughter – Natalie. Sadly, Mrs. Seizen eventually died which was no surprise as her health had been ailing so many months. At her funeral I asked her for a sign that she existed in the afterlife, and everything was okay with her, but none came that day. The next week her cleaning lady went to help her son Tommy go through her possessions. Mrs. Seizen's son - Tommy - came over to her and said, "I just found money in one of my mom's shirts and as I was putting it in my wallet, Mrs. Feingate stopped me and said no - no - you give that to Irene. She only put money in her pocket for Irene."

Tommy, my boss – came to work and said he had something for me. It was $10 - as his mother had always gave me. I became emotional receiving yet another confirmation of life after death. "Tommy, your mom's okay," I smiled and hugged him.

I have had a great life. Occasionally I do float or fly in dreams – it's amazing! Is this astral travel? I think so. I have learned to maneuver flight by balancing my breathing and hand movements. Sometimes it's easier than others. One night I was having a hard time lifting off and asked, "Why can't I do it tonight?" and a clear voice stated, "You're too fat." I laughed myself awake at that point. Still laughing at that. Who the hell said that?

Another time, I was sleeping and dreaming and see a bunch of clouds from Heaven – like a huge storm was coming – *Wizard Of Oz* dramatic clouds - the clouds landed on the ground - all of a sudden the dark clouds started opening up – the clouds inside were very white – I look inside and in the distance – and I can see how far it goes and then all the way down I see men – in robes - like Moses - crowds of people all the way down – women too - feels and looks so beautiful – layered in goose bumps – I want to go in and be a part of that – and just as I am about to step into the clouds, a Cherubic little blond boy stops me and says, "Not yet, Irene – it's not your time."

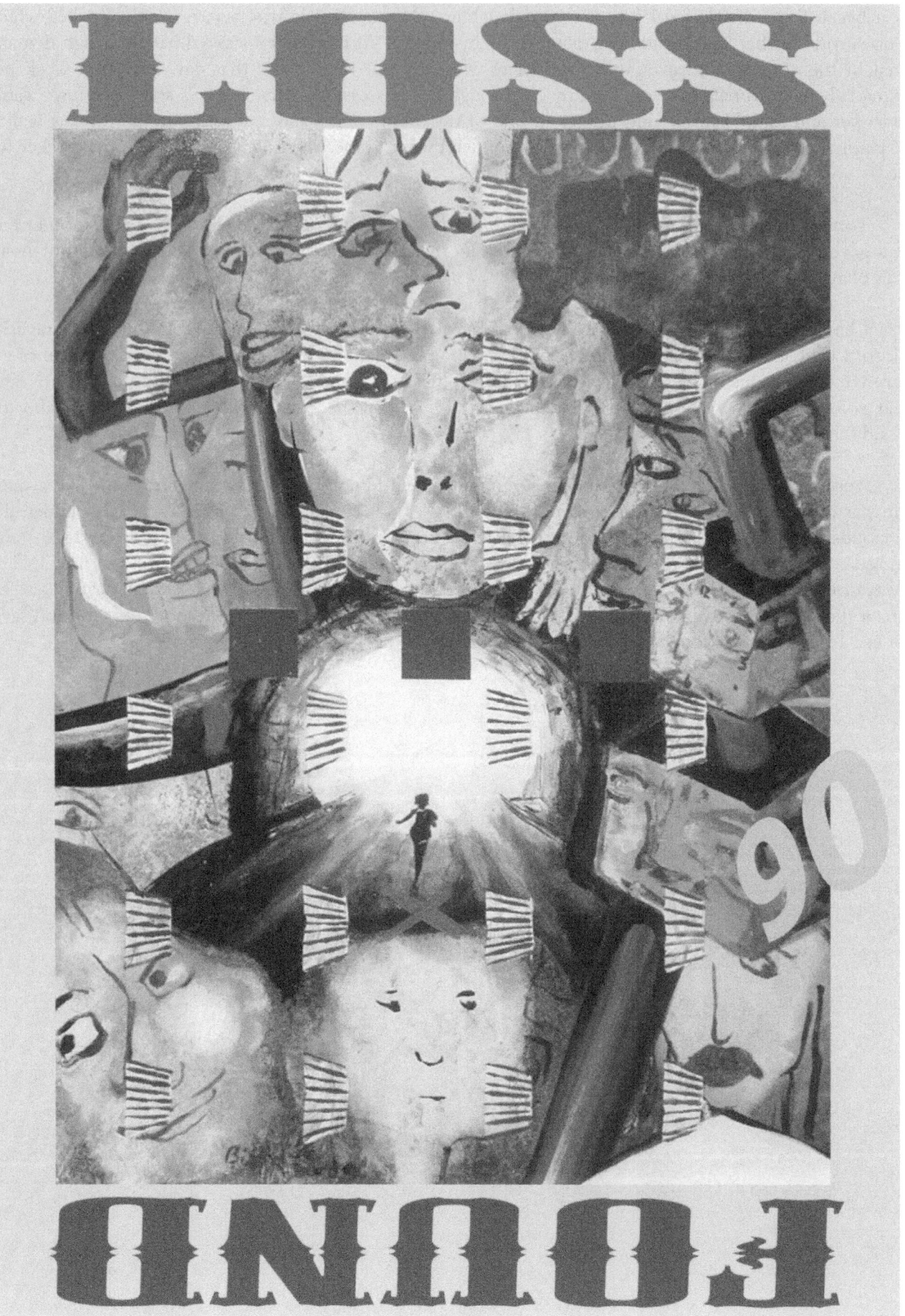

CHAPTER 8   PARENTS DANCING BETWEEN DIMENSIONS

by Mike M.

My family was a crazy Italian family that was very dysfunctional, but loving… or loving enough. The home we lived in was a row house in the suburbs of Philadelphia called Clifton Heights. I was 25 when my parents died. My father died of cancer in 1981 and my mother died of lung infection complicated by gangrene in her intestines in 1982. She was co-dependent on my father and really died from a broken heart at 60. Because I was an only child, after they died, I moved back into their home; my childhood home.

I would start to see visions in my room, especially my parents dancing in front of the bed. It was strange because they never danced when they were alive. The images were not clear to me. There were just 2 people in front of the bed dancing. This happened many times. One night, I saw my pants and shirt move across the room. I thought I had dreamed this, but when I woke up, the pants which had been on the chair by the window, were now on the floor in front of the bed.

At the time I didn't know about spirits coming back to be with you. My memories of my hometown were not good ones. Growing up there was difficult because I was picked on.

After I moved to Florida, things still happened. I had a roommate who said my parents' ghosts were in the bedroom where she was. It totally freaked her out. Not knowing what this was and being young, I had someone, a friend of my roommates, come in and do an exorcism.

This was the worst thing I could have done. After this, I had terrible luck for many years. I think my parents were there to protect me.

Last year, my longtime partner, Peter, died Thanksgiving Day. Two days after he died, I was walking from the kitchen to the bedroom and so help me God; he was laying in our bed looking at me. I know he was there. I was walking to the bedroom from the kitchen. It was just a moment that I saw him there. He was lying on the bed in shorts looking at me. It touched me deeply. It made me feel like he was there to protect me.

Peter and I had vacationed every year to Florida since 1995. The first year we got a great room. It was a partial ocean view room which had a view of the Miami skyline and the pool. It was a perfect room. In 2001 new owners took over the hotel and would not assign any special rooms so we never got this room again. Last week when I checked in, I was given the same room 938 after 7 years. I never asked for it or thought about it. What's that about?

CHAPTER 9   LEAVING HER BODY DURING MOLESTATION

by Deb Hagler Wong

It is often more difficult to open up about metaphysical stuff than to discuss anything else. There is always the risk of ridicule, loss of credibility, or being seen as "flaky".

For myself, anyone who knows me well knows about my numerous out of body / astral projection experiences as a child. I had no control over these incidents, which happened at least once a month or so. Often they happened during times of trauma, like when my father was abusing me.

I was a shy kid, friendly with only those that I could trust, which were few. I was about 7 or 8 when the out-of-body experiences started. I had not heard of such things, but I did grow up Catholic, so wasn't completely unaware of the metaphysical. I lived in Pacifica, Ca. (am a 5th generation native San Franciscan). I was the oldest of nine kids altogether, and was responsible for taking care of the youngest six, in addition to the housework (along with my sister), which included my father's laundry, shoe polishing, & everyone else's laundry, too. Everything had to be done right. Ironing is still a problem for me, because I would have to stand at the ironing board for hours until every single wrinkle was out. If the bed wasn't made, shoes not polished, etc., we were beaten severely, always with sticks, electrical cords or other implements, always either with our clothes off or pants down. There had to be humiliation in the process. Once when the dishes weren't clean enough, my hands were put under scalding water. The week after that, the skin on my hands peeled, which was a cause of shame for me.

There was always terrible pain, and terror. We older kids just lived in terror. My father was a sheet metal worker, who was a Golden Gloves boxer on TV for a while. He punched us with his boxer's hands. My mom was a keypunch operator and worked nights, slept days. She became an alcoholic, so was able to blind herself from things she did not want to see.

Often these out-of-body experiences happened during times of trauma, like when my father was raping or beating me. No my father didn't drink (mom did, though). He DID have a lot of rage.....which was odd, because he could do anything that he wanted. All through his marriage to my mom, he had other women on the side. In fact, my sister & I contracted a venereal disease that he had gotten from one of his women (mom was faithful all throughout her marriage - the good Catholic). My father had a dermatologist friend who gave Laurie (my sister) & I shots for it; I think that it was penicillin. My father always had expensive toys - airplanes, boats, nice guitars & amps (he was a back-up musician for a lot of famous people who came through San Francisco). He later wrote in a letter to me - which I also can provide - that he was a "different man" when young, was enraged about my mom having so many kids. It was a lame apology letter, especially with the timing of it (long story). Basically, I think that he was a sociopath, and a pathological liar. He would lie about anything & everything. He also never could empathize with anyone else. When he was in pain, he howled, but he never felt anyone else's pain.

I didn't have control of the out-of-body experiences - it would have been great if I could. The pains from the rapes (which initially started when I was 8, and ended when I was 17) were excruciating. I still have the medical report of my injuries. I contacted the hospital when I was in my 30s, to get that report, because I needed to have that validation. My father would tell anyone and everyone that I was a liar, that I made up stories - this was how he protected himself. This was how he was able to continue his crimes all of those years. You have to understand that this was back in the 50s & 60s and people just didn't talk about those kinds of things. I didn't even know what it was that he was doing to me. He threatened my sister and I that if we ever told anyone about what was going on, he would kill us, cut us up and throw us in the ocean. Other threats had to do with cutting up our faces so that no one would ever want to look at us again. We knew that he was capable of it. That is why we kept our mouths shut. I learned to keep quiet, even in pain.

If you check out the damage on the report, you can see that I had to endure a lot. In later years, I opened up about this, had some of my writing on it published a local newspaper, and was told that it helped to discuss this.

When I was 11, I was in a car accident where our car's breaks went out on top of a steep hill. I have two newspaper clippings about it. We were on our way to church, at the top of steep Manor Drive. My brother Arlo was in the front seat, my sister Laurie & I in the back, and Mom was driving. She drove like a champ. Didn't hit a thing or person. The car was a 1951 Studebaker. They don't make 'em like that anymore. I am convinced that if it was something that is made today with that cheap metal, I would not be here writing this!

Going down the hill, early morning, sunny weather - June 23, 1963. Lots of houses on both sides, so not many people out. My Mom had us say the "Act of Contrition", the prayer that Catholics say just before they die, so that they can get into Heaven. Arlo was in the front seat, holding on, and screaming. Laurie was on the floor in the back seat (and had the most injuries). Mom had a cut finger that needed to be stitched. I had pieces of glass in parts of my body (this was the old type of car glass). I still have two scars from where the glass penetrated in my legs. But nothing major.

I tried not to look, was busy holding onto the back of the seat (no seatbelts back then). I saw a few people staring at us, sort of in shock, on our way down. When we neared the beach, I held on tighter, and then recall the Studebaker flipping 3 times. I counted. I heard nothing. At that moment, I floated up, and saw our car below, and it occurred to me that I was dead. It was quite peaceful. Then I was back on the ground, on the sand, in shock that there was sound again - and I was looking for a small stuffed animal, a leopard, that I called "Leopard Cue-Cue", and was upset that I couldn't find him. My mom, sister & brother were sitting on a sand dune, and there were people all around. Laurie had blood on her head. Someone said to get away from the car, as there was a gas leak, and the car might explode. A nice lady came out to us with blankets, and covered us with them, while we waited for the ambulance.

Sometimes my out-of-body experiences happened when there was no drama or trauma. I would be walking with a friend, and then suddenly be outside of my body, watching myself. Not sure WHY this happened at these times. I didn't feel threatened. I couldn't control it, had no warning when it would occur.

Once I was walking with my best friend down Inverness Drive, after school (by the way, I am still in touch with this best friend, who lives in West Hollywood - a fellow artist who worked on the *Simpson's* cartoon show for a while. But I digress). I was suddenly on the outside, looking at us both. It only happened for a few seconds, and then I was back in my body. She thought that I just wasn't listening - and I wasn't.

This happened several times at school, once outside my desk. Most of the time, just before it happens, everything in my vision kind of goes red. It feels a lot like deja vu', which I have experienced many times (that is a much more common experience). I know this is a clumsy description, but it has not happened to me in decades, so I am relying on memory. I did think after awhile - when I discovered that my friends didn't talk about going through this stuff - that there was something wrong with me. I mean, I KNEW there was something wrong with me, anyway, because my father wouldn't have acted the way that he did if I was OK. That was what I believed as a child.

One thing that I do know is that when I was not in my body, my hearing was muffled or non-existent. Sight is everywhere; you can control what you want to see for immeasurable distances with just a thought. But hearing is muffled. At least it was for me. It has nothing to do with boredom, but my mind itself did wander a lot. I loved to draw, just entered the paper with my pencils, and "lived" there.

When I was 10, I was hospitalized (from injuries due to one of the rapes). The medical report is available. I was raped the night of January 8, 1962. To preface this, my father raped me once or twice a week; my sister Laurie (and later my sister Sue) was also raped. It started out with molestation; as far back as I can remember. Tongue kissing, having to touch him and perform oral, etc.. It was like the other punishments, only worse, because there was an element that I can't describe - that part that is too personal. That and the fact that in Catholicism, that part of the body was just not mentioned. My mother was very repressed in that way (oddly enough - after having nine kids), and never spoke to us except to say that it was bad. I had mixed messages all throughout my childhood about sex. I even went to confession, and told the Father that I was an adulteress (I was 13), as I had read that any woman who has sex with another woman's husband is a sinner. Father came out of the confessional after that and put his arm around me, saying that I must be mistaken. All I know is that I didn't like Father touching me.

In any event, on that rape night, my father told me to go into the bedroom. It was always a time of fear. He instructed me to lie on the bed and remove my panties, as per usual. But this time, instead of stopping with partial penetration, he kept going all the way. I cried out, and he hit me in the face, and then put his hand over my mouth, so that my screams could not be heard. The pain was the WORST. When he tore me completely (read the report), I was hemorrhaging, and I asked him if I was going to die. He ran around looking for a towel, and was trying to clean up as much as he could of the evidence. He said that he "didn't know" (and of course didn't care, except for the consequences where he was concerned). I WISH I could have left my body at that point, but didn't until after I got to the hospital. He got one of my mother's sanitary napkins for me to wear (I had never seen one before - that is how ignorant I was - and wondered about that. He called my mother, who was at work, and told her & everyone else that I had been playing pogo stick with the toilet plunger. He even smeared blood on the tip of it. The doctor and one of the nuns (this was a Catholic hospital) asked me how the injury occurred, and I didn't say anything. As weird as it sounds, I was embarrassed by the whole situation, and fearful of being killed if the truth got out. But after my father told them about my playing pogo stick - which if you looked at the height of the stick, my height, the time of night when it occurred (11:30 PM.), etc. you can see how ridiculous that was - I was even teased by a couple nurses for doing something so "childish". Back then, people didn't examine those things too much. If it were today, things would be very different. In any event, it was humiliating having to spread my legs for the doctor & nurses.

And as I waited for the doctor to show up, I floated up, and looked down at my body, which appeared to be sleeping. Perhaps I had passed out from blood loss. My consciousness decided that I wanted to leave the room, so I went through the wall. As I was floating outside, I was suddenly blinded by a white light, a presence which told me (not in words but in "thoughts") that I had to stay behind, that I couldn't go home yet.

There was the implication that we are all here for a purpose, and when we are done with that, and then we can return to our original home. I felt a pressurized pulling force on me (hard to describe). It felt like a strong vacuum, suctioning force, pulling on your whole body. As with so much else, I had no control over that. The home that the Light Being spoke of was our "true" home. What the spirit or angel implied was that we are here for a reason, and that I am not done yet. I didn't feel relief at that, it was almost "Oh no, I have to go through more." And was then back in my body. Softly, gently. I was never aware of the exact instant. It was like: *I'm outside of my body. Now I'm back in.* Not a sudden slap, just a gentle: "Here I am". The only "warning" was prior to leaving the body, that red vision thing.

I was stitched up with catgut, and the stitches had to be removed a week after I left the hospital (I was in there for 11 days).

I couldn't shake the idea that I had been in the love and presence of my Guardian Angel. It was just a powerful Being of Light. It had been next to me, with a very reassuring and protective presence. Since it was a brief encounter, there wasn't much more to it, except what I can only call "implications" about our purpose here. I do remember quite vividly thinking: *"Of COURSE. I knew about this already. How could I have forgotten?"*

I never told anyone at the time about this, except my best friend, who laughed and thought I was joking so I knew to keep quiet.

Here is an aside about that time: It was the first year of my life when it snowed in San Francisco, and I wasn't even able to play in the snow. I had never seen snow. My siblings kept a couple of snowballs for me in the freezer, for when I came home from the hospital. I appreciated that, but of course felt left out. Another note: My 4th grade classmates all wrote get well soon letters to me. One of them was the man who was to become my husband many years later.

On another paranormal note, I have had prophetic dreams - some of which were rather startling in their accuracy & timing - but they were few & far between.

One day when I was 32, I had a vivid dream that my daughter (who was 12 at the time) was going to start her first period. The next morning, I told her, my sister and my (then) husband about it, and my daughter scoffed at me. Later in the day, my daughter came running to me that she had just started her period. Mind you, I was surrounded by skeptics, who thought that it was a weird coincidence. I have had MANY of those, so many I can't go into specifics.

Another memorable vivid dream was when my grandfather came to me, and told me that he was "leaving the neighborhood," and that he was going to be with Grandma, and that I wouldn't see him for a while. It was a very sad dream - I woke up crying. Two days later, my sister asked me if I was going to the funeral. I asked her, "Who died?"

"Didn't anybody tell you? Grandpa died."

He had passed away the very day that I had the dream. It is now part of family folklore.

I found that science explained my astral projection experiences as "disassociation," where brain chemistry is altered during crises, and one essentially hallucinates. But something within me just "knows" that what I went through was real.

I think the brain is our "excuse" for what we can already do - our repository. Flesh is the container, for lack of a better description. My daughter, who is an atheist, and only believes what science teaches, scoffs at my thinking. But I know what I know. Science is great, it's tangible, but so very limited.

I stopped having the experiences when I was about 14. I am not entirely sure why, but I had many things going against me at the time. It was bad enough that I was not believed when I tried to tell a few people about what my father was doing to me. One teacher said: "Deborah - every girl wants to marry their father. That doesn't make it true."

So, it would be unrewarding, to say the least, to continue exiting the carcass, so to speak. Another is possibly that I was maturing, and had so many other considerations. We are also brought up in a culture that does not welcome speaking about the metaphysical as if it were real. It's okay in films or books, but not in reality. My father threatened to put me in a mental hospital (as my brother Mark has been in - he is autistic) for most of his life. But truly - it wasn't conscious. It just stopped happening.

One of my artworks includes my sister Laurie & brother Arlo, both of whom have passed on (Laurie in a car accident at 16, Arlo of cancer at 48). I am sitting on the shore....I call it "Reflections."

My husband & I are both artists, but also custom framers, and understand the pressures of putting up a gallery show, both for ourselves and other artists.

As far as what I went through in my childhood – the unexplainable – WHY – I have no idea. I do know that there are many others who have been through worse. Perhaps I needed to learn some lessons here. It is the most reasonable and acceptable explanation to me. That everyone in our lives, good and bad, is part of that lesson. How it has it made me the person I am today? Too much to tell. To say that I had trust issues would be an understatement. But I developed empathy for others that I possibly would not have had otherwise. The pain also honed my sense of humor. Sounds strange, but true. My imagination was developed when I was young, as well, partly as an escape from "the real world" as it was. And I have always been spiritual, in spite of being surrounded by non-believers for most of my adult life. My early brief astral projection experiences were a blessing in that way.

You know, I have always been an artist. In fact, my husband Michael used to love to watch me draw horses when we were kids. I haven't had as much time for artworks creation lately - too much on my plate - but even in my photo restoration work, animation creations, websites, there is creation. I never went to college after high school (married when I was 19 and 5 months pregnant), so I am self-taught in everything (including teaching myself Spanish), so I feel very grateful that people are actually paying me to do these jobs that I love to do. And I know that my loved ones on the other side are looking out for me, as I will do for my loved ones when I leave this body - for good.

One thing I forgot to mention about that car crash I was in when I was 11. When I got first into the car, before our trip, I said: "This is the first time I have ever been in this car...and the last." WHY I said that I hadn't a clue, (turned out to be prophetic), and my sister told me that was a dumb thing to say. But it is indicative of premonitions that I have had throughout life. Words come out of my mouth without thought, then it happens. Weird.

Deb can be contacted at https://springmountaingallery.com/

CHAPTER 10   BOY GETS NIGHTLY ADVICE FROM GRANDMA'S GHOST

by Adrian

On 9/11, I had one of those dreams where I was dreaming and didn't know it. Meaning that I had my night dream, and then I thought I had woke up but I was still dreaming. I have lots of those dreams, where I thought I had woken up and but actually was still dreaming. I was getting up to go to work at MGM. And when I left I walked into my apartment parking area and there were burnt cars. I thought it was weird but I just walked around them. I knew it was odd for them to be there, but I had to get to work. My car was not seen as it was parking on a side street. I had to walk through the lot to get to it. I could smell the burnt cars. And then I realized I left my wallet in my apartment and so I walked back to my apt, opened the door and just woke up.

As soon as I opened my front door, I was back in my bed awake. The thought in my head was, "Oh great, not again." I have had the dream of waking up and getting ready for work. Where the same just repeats. I was just unsure of the time. Which is probably why I turned on the TV, for the morning news and time, and then I saw the planes strike the towers. I went outside and the parking garage was empty, as the seven neighbors had left for work.

On a side note, something my mom could verify. When I was little, like four, at night I would get up and go the living room to talk with my Mom's grandmother who was very loving and caring. I thought she lived with us. She was very old. I'd talk to her about my day, she would tell me how to behave, and how not to. My thinking was that she was available nights for our talks because she must have worked in the day. I was just four. What did I know? My parents had day jobs. Mom worked as a secretary and dad at Kaiser Steel. So to me it was normal to expect adults home in the late afternoon. I just thought that was the same case for my grandmother. So at night, when my parents were asleep, I would get up from bed and go to the living room and my grandmother would always be there in the dark. So I would talk with her. It wasn't until 2nd grade when I learned she had died in 1971. Three years before I was born!

Describing the dear old woman, my Mom affirmed it was my grandmother. They were very close. I still remember seeing her after I was told she was dead, and pretending to myself that I didn't know what my mom told me.

But when I told Mom, Mom just told me that in our house only our family lived there, and that our grandmother did not. She reiterated to me that grandma died several years before, and for me to tell her whenever I saw her ghost. Mom would ask me what we would talk about.

Our conversations were always nice. Stories about herself, about telling me how to understand my parents. How I should behave or shouldn't in different situations (meaning if my dad got mad at me, how I needed to understand what I did wrong, or what he was doing wrong and how not to provoke him). Growing up my dad drank A LOT. There were lots of fights, but I distinctly remember being told how he was going through hard times at work and didn't know how to handle the pressure. I would tell grandmother about school. But I was never afraid of her. But after I knew she was dead and I was still seeing her, then she would look like a ghost, meaning she glowed. But I was never afraid, I was fascinated.

I know not everyone has the same thoughts when it comes to this. I don't think I invented her presence. I have always believed in spirits, ghosts, reincarnation. Always. Which is why I got bored going to church. My mom encouraged me to learn about all religions and for me to develop my own beliefs. I am the third child of four children. But for seven years I was the baby of the family until my sister arrived. The last time I remember seeing her was in high school. My mom would always find me on the couch, looking suspicious, and just ask me about it.

I don't really pray to my grandmother. I think I have spirit guides that watch over me, which really come in handy when I feel alone. I kind of talk to my guides before I go to sleep, I always thank them and always give my word of how I am going to act. And in return they give me positive words, and encouragement. I do not think I imagine this. They have helped me out of so many situations and encouraged me to do so much on blind faith. (Like when it came to producing stage shows, and even a pilot I produced.)

I know that my brother's son sees stuff. Once again, he tells my mom what he saw. I think it was about two years ago, she called me and asked me if her grandmother was still there in the house. I was like, "I have no idea." And she told me that little Brian might have seen her and Mom was fascinated by that.

I believe energy doesn't die. It just transforms. A perfect example of energy changing is an ice cube can turn to water, water can turn to vapor and gas, and that vapor/gas turns into water, and that can turn into a solid piece of ice. So that's some of what I think.

CHAPTER 11   EERILY ESCAPING DISASTER AFTER DISASTER

by Ben

Nothing ever happens to me - I get there and miss all the action but I am there.

High school, Lilac Festival, Mount St Helen erupts – I was unscratched.

Murrah building, show up for a tax question in college, leave 10 minutes later – I escaped right before the Oklahoma City Bombing.

NYC, started the job at MTA, Sept 4. I go to work Sept 11, thru the Jersey side path tunnel, the World Trade Center disaster happens but I emerge form it fine.

Three days after 9/11, my assignment is down by Union Square, scaffolding falls across the street. People next to me are hurt from the debris, but nothing hits me.

One time twenty-minutes after I finish eating dinner across from the museum, the Philadelphia, pier collapses.

I did military service in Afghanistan. People around me got shot. Me: nothing.

Way back when I was a teen, I get grounded, which saved my life because that night my best friend died as he and our other friend flipped the Toyota in the ice. The friend who died was sitting in my normal; seat.

I used to feel guilty about this stuff.

Maybe I am like a watcher or a person who is supposed to record it?

I have friends who joke that in the case of a disaster, I am the person to stand closest to.

CHAPTER 12   GRANDMOTHER CROSSED THE LINE, LITERALLY

by Miss Priss

Okay... this is kind of strange, but it happened to me in a dream, and I have never forgotten it either. When I was a sophomore in high school, I took a class trip to Washington D.C.. Before I left, I had spoken to my grandmother, who had a surgical procedure scheduled to have her veins stripped. It wasn't supposed to be anything life-threatening, but while I was gone on the trip she had a stroke in the hospital. All of my family and extended family were there to talk to her, and to say "goodbye" as things were not looking good. She died while I was gone.

Her visitation was on my birthday. I always felt bad that I never had the opportunity to say goodbye. One night - probably a year (or maybe even two) later I had a dream where an older well-known couple from my home town came up to me. They told me that Grandma was going to come and say goodbye to me - but I needed to tell her what I needed to because once she "stepped back over the line" she would be gone and I would never see her again. I agreed....

All of a sudden, my Grandma came walking across this yellow line on the floor into the shower of light (the spotlight) that I was standing in. I gave her a kiss and hug, told her I loved her and good-bye - she told me she loved me back, and then walked back over the line.

Suddenly I was awake in my bed with an unbelievable calm and sense of peace. I have never forgotten that dream or the feeling of peace that gave me. That happened over 30 years ago, and I still picture it like it just happened.

Now with my mom gone, I look for her - but she hasn't come to me in my dreams...yet.

CHAPTER 13   PAPA AS MY RECURRING GUARDIAN ANGEL

by Kerri-Anne Rider MacFarlane

I now live in Edmonton, Alberta, Canada, but was raised in homey Huntsville, Ontario, Canada. Leonard Rider, my grandfather who I called Papa, looked like JFK to me; tall, handsome, dark hair with brown eyes.

Papa is my spirit guide. He passed when I was six years old of a heart attack. He has been visiting me and talking to me since I was a child. I don't usually see him. I just feel him and hear him, in a quiet, normal voice - but sometimes that clairaudient channel seems obstructed and I have to figure out his messages with telepathy.

Papa lets me know when something terrible is going to happen or when someone is sick, so I can warn people. He probably also does this because I have been considered over-emotional and maybe he is relaxing me into painful changes. A feeling will just come over me and I know he is trying to tell me something. I stop, sit and listen. With his guidance I can sometimes let people know, to not go for that drive, etc..

Papa alerted me when my dog was going to die. He also told me my best friend Lorie Mcknight was going to pass away, quite unexpectedly - but I didn't know a date and couldn't save her. I asked her to be careful. I suggested she change her daily activities. She had epilepsy and had not had a grand mal seizure in years. Papa warned me it was going to happen. The day my wolf Yukon died, Lorie, passed away at the same moment.

Papa warned me about my father-in-law: he showed me a picture of blood running down his legs. Turns out he got super sick and ended up in the hospital with back and lung issues. Fortunately, he got help before it got worse.

On a hot July night in 2009, I woke to an awful feeling; a feeling I had received from Papa: someone very close to me was going to die. I was so upset that there came no name - so couldn't warn anyone in particular. After a few days I just let it go, but when I did, in less than a week the same feeling kept coming over me. Soon I felt this in the daylight and it would not go away. I tried to figure out who it was but I had no idea. Was it my husband Michael – or one of our kids?!

In the beginning of September, I had a dream where Papa told me it was my father. I was devastated and didn't want to believe it. I called my parents' house and spoke to my ma who had just found out my dad had gone to the doc without her knowledge to have tests done. The next day my dad called me and said he had stomach cancer and he only had a short time to be with us on this earth.

My daddy was tall with dark hair, he had what we call the Rider eye, one eye had kind of a slant - my brother and I have the same eyes. Dad loved to smoke his pipe, or cigars, drink cognac and martinis. He was a very hard working man who owned many business and even ran for mayor of Huntsville one year, only missing by a handful of votes. Though he was busy I never felt cheated on time or gifts. In fact, every year since I was a tot he got me one rose for Valentine's Day. And I dried them and saved them – still have them.

Every other day between September and May I phoned my parents. On May 26, 2010, I knew I had to fly home to be with daddy, because my spirit guide Papa again had come to see me. When I called to make flight arrangements, daddy answered, affirming, "It is time to come home." I was broken in so many ways, I am his little girl, his peanut. He was my rock through my life. I was on the plane the next day.

When I awoke at my parents' home, there was a deer in the backyard. There are lots of deer but you don't see them in town limits very often. If you do, they leave ASAP, but oddly, this beautiful deer whom I called Hope, never left the back door - until three weeks later when my daddy's soul left his body. She has never been seen again.

June 17, 2010. It was my night up with my dad who had gone from 170 lbs. to only 90. Mom and my brother were asleep in their rooms. I turned the TV off. Dad and I sat in the living room in the dark. He breathed heavy, looked at me and said, "Peanut, it's time for me to close my eyes. I am exhausted and cannot fight any more."

Daddy and me.

With tears in our eyes, we hugged. When I got up to guide him to his room, he asked me to open the sliding glass door to let some air in. I did - and yes the deer was still there watching us. When I opened the door, Papa appeared in a mist. Not a wet mist but a fog mist. I smiled and his body shape became defined. He touched me. I felt his love, it was like he was hugging me. I could hear in my mind him saying, "I am here now to take the pain away." I felt peace come over me but at the same time so much sadness.

I nodded, "It's time for you to take daddy home with you."

At that very moment, Papa glided through the open door. His foggy spirit went past me, exhilarating my soul - and then he went to his son, holding out his hand. Unaware of any of this, Daddy said he was ready for bed. I took him in and nestled him in blankets and pillows. He muttered, "I love you, Peanut." With tears flowing down his cheeks he slipped into a coma that night.

June 19: I told my family I was going to go out for the night with friends and relax by the firepit where my children grew up. We sang songs, we laughed, we cried. My heart was heavy because I knew I would not see my father again.

June 20: at 12.19 AM. A few minutes into Father's Day, we were still sitting by the fire. I slumped in my chair and felt my daddy's soul touch my shoulders. One of my dearest friends, Jeremy, looked up from his guitar and said, "Ker, there is a huge ball of light over you!"

Closing my eyes I breathed deep. I said, "I know my daddy is now an angel."

At this time, my girlfriend took a picture and you can see his light all over me.

I went through the photos from the moment my dad passed and this is one we cannot explain. There were no other photos like this - just this one - the others were normal.

This photo was taken when my friend Jeremy said Ker there is a light over you, not sure if can see if but it looks like a very tall man standing beside them.

June 27: My husband, Michael, who had arrived a few days before, and I boarded a plane to come back to Edmonton, Alberta. After a couple of weeks of depression, I begged for Papa to send Daddy to me just one more time. Dad's cologne awoke me. He was sitting on the side of my bed - so real I actually thought he was alive. I saw him like he was still here - not an angel, but he had regained his weight and looked perfectly healthy. The light surrounding him was the most beautiful, incredible light I have ever seen, it was HEAVEN - there was an aura around him. As my husband slept soundly, Dad held my hand and spoke, saying he was sorry he had to leave so early in his life, at only 62 years old. He said that he will always be here when I need him. He then kissed my hand and turned around and I watched him slowly turn into the foggy mist I saw when Papa walked in the sliding glass door. My father turned back one more time, smiled, waved and disappeared into the light.

It has been 9 years since he got his wings. I am blessed to have a gift to see and speak to the angels. They are never far away.

Recently, seeing just for fun if he would come whenever I needed, I called him and the seat cushion beside me sunk down, as if there was weight making the impression, and I smelled his cologne. I was just having have a convo with him and he throws one the roses I saved from my wall unit to my shoes! About 5 feet!

CHAPTER 14   DEAD FATHER FINDS THEM A PERFECT APARTMENT

by Kathy

It was late April, 1971, in a small town in Indiana. My husband and I were recently married, searching for an apartment and living with his mom at the time, staying in his old room.

For many years, I had been told of visits to the house from his late dad. My husband was twelve when his dad passed. The story was always the same: it would be in the wee hours of the morning, the hallway light would come on and my husband's bedroom door would open. He would feel a touch on his foot and he would know his dad was there and something good would be happening soon, things like, a new job, acceptance to college, etc., just normal everyday occurrences.

On this particular Saturday night, I was in bed on the side closest to the door and suddenly woke up. I could see the light under the door from the hallway, but I didn't think anything about it as his brothers still lived at home and his mom was home as well. Something seemed "off" though, so I laid very still and listened. No sounds at all. Then the bedroom door opened slightly, but no one appeared in the doorway. I waited quietly and then felt the slightest pressure on my ankle. I turned to my husband and said, "Honey, your dad is here." He woke up right away, but not soon enough. By then the door was slowly closing and the hallway went dark.

Everyone in the house was so excited as I recounted the details over and over for them. Then at 1:30 on that Sunday afternoon when all businesses were closed, the phone rang. It was a realtor, who we had never talked to or had ever dealt with, calling to tell my mother-in-law about an apartment that had just become available. She asked him how he knew that her son and I were hunting for a new residence. He said he had received a message to call when one became available. He didn't know who left the message, but it had her phone number.

We left to meet him right away and it was perfect! A first-hand experience for me that the stories I had heard over the years happened exactly as described.

CHAPTER 15 TOMATO-LOVING FATHER DIES, LEAVES A SURPRISE

by Edwina

My Dad, Eddie B, who everyone knew around our neighborhood, was a US Navy, WWII Vet. He passed away Sept.30, 2006.

Always had a favorite saying: "When I'm dead and buried, you can tear it down." "It" meaning the very old shed in the back of our house.

When Dad was around we wanted to make the yard livable. But Dad couldn't part with this shed of his, having had built it with his dad. Grandfathers initials are carved in the wood from the inside of the door.

Well, during Dad's life he loved to plant tomatoes. We had a full yard of grass and needless to say, tomatoes were not favored in our yard. So, Dad would buy ready-made tomato plants and plant them that way. They never grew to a full size tomato, some came out with only three small fruits.

I really felt bad for Dad because even at 87 years-old he worked so hard at this.

Time went on and summers came and went and we decided to pave one side of the yard since nothing was growing. A few years went by and Dad eventually left this world.

Six months later, March of 2007, I saw a stem coming out from the side of the shed, which I took pictures of it. This was a tomato plant that came from under the rotten shed that we were going to tear down.

How can we do this when this miracle tomato plant was growing from UNDER the shed? Tomatoes that couldn't and wouldn't grow when Dad was living. Was this a sign?

Sure it was. Like Dad still saying, "Don't tear down the shed! And enjoy the tomatoes from up above."

We had at least 120! Every day I felt my dad was still in that backyard doing his planting. It wasn't a feeling of, "Oh! I have to take care of that plant now."

It was a spiritual feeling of touching my dad's heart when removing the tomatoes.

My mom, who is 89 now, would run upstairs with the tomatoes and she just had a glow about her knowing that her husbands' being was still around us. I even think the tomatoes tasted different, sweeter.

CHAPTER 16   HAUNTED HOUSE TURNS ON NEW OWNERS

by R.S.

About 13 years ago my husband mike and I were still renovating and flipping old homes down in the Leslieville area of Toronto. We had just sold a house and were out looking with our real estate agent David who was also a very good friend to us. We were viewing this one house at 37 Kyntyre Ave which was an estate sale.

The owner of the home was an elderly lady named Libby who had inherited the house from her parents who had passed. As we went thru the house, I kept saying, "Let's go. I'm not interested in it." But Mike kept insisting we go thru the whole house.

As we proceeded the viewing I kept feeling this heaviness in the air like it was hard to breathe and I hated the house. To me, there was nothing appealing to it - I didn't see that you could do a lot with it. But Mike kept saying he had to have this house, he didn't know why but something was telling him to buy this house.

When we got home that night, Mike was still insisting on this house. He finally used the card, "You picked the last one. Let me pick this one." I finally gave in and said okay because he was desperate for this house.

The next day we put the offer in and was accepted immediately. We were running out of time as our old house was about to close in two weeks so we asked for a quick closing which the son to Libby agreed,

A couple of days later after all the paperwork was done and signed, our agent, David, gave us the keys to the house to go in and measure the windows as they had to be replaced right away. He just asked us to be very quiet not to let people see us in there as it wasn't legally our house yet.

Mike and I go to the house in the middle of the day, and we were not comfortable being there so Mike suggested we leave and come back at night when no one's around. I said to Mike, "Let me call David and see if that's okay."

I went to use the phone in the house that was sitting on the coffee table, but the phone had no dial tone, so we just left and arranged with David to go back that night, which we did. Mike went downstairs to check the furnace and I measured the windows in the living room. On the window ledge was this tiny crystal unicorn. Because Libby was dead, I didn't think she would mind if I took her unicorn.

The minute I put that unicorn in my pocket the landline phone started to ring. Not only did it ring - there was a red light on the phone that was blinking. I guessed Libby was hard of hearing so the light let her know the phone was ringing? I couldn't believe the phone was ringing because it was completely dead earlier that day. I picked up the phone and it was completely dead, no dial tone – nothing!

At that time I took the unicorn and put it back on the window ledge. Something in that house did not want me there.

A minute later, Mike came running up the basement stairs saying to me, "What the f&ck are you doing banging on the basement window yelling my name?!" I told him, "Mike, I haven't left the living room." I then told him about the phone ringing.

We just stood there for a minute. Finally Mike says we're just being nuts, so we ignored what was happening and went upstairs to measure the windows there. As Mike measured I sat on the edge of the bed and I could literally feel myself BEING PUSHED OFF THE BED.

I jumped up and yelled, "I'm getting the fuck out of here!" Mike replied, "I'm going, too. I can't frickin breathe in here."

We both got our stuff together and started to leave and as we were locking up the house I said to Mike that whatever is in there doesn't want us there and this deal is gonna fall thru. As we were leaving, the neighbor was on his front porch, and started a conversation with us, telling us all about Libby and how she had lived there her entire life and the last year or so, her son wanted her to go to assisted living but she just would not leave this house. She finally died in the living room a few weeks prior.

The very next morning, David called and said the son wanted to keep the house and if we would consider cancelling the deal. Mike and I both said absolutely, not a problem. Truth be told, we were up the whole night before trying to figure out how to get out of this deal.

Two years later I'm driving home from work and listening to the news. A contractor had just bought a home at 37 Kyntyre Avenue and was renovating, ripping out walls - and found the remains of a new born baby that had been mummified. They figured the baby corpse was about 75 years old.

Mike and I watched the late night news and were not shocked at all. We knew at the time something was going on in that house. The son of Libby made a statement that he had heard rumors that Libby as a teenager had become pregnant, but he didn't know what had happened to the baby. Mike and I kind of thought when Libby gave birth. the baby was still born, or Libby's parents murdered the baby because of the times back then - we all know what people thought of unwed mothers. But whatever happened someone put that baby in the wall.

The contractor paid for a cemetery plot for the baby and is buried nearby. Whatever happened though I'm sure it was Libby there that night... angry I took her unicorn!

But in the end, the newborn baby was laid to rest – finally - after 75 years.

Morals of the story: don't steal from the dead. Always listen to your gut when something is telling you that something isn't right. It's usually because something isn't right.

CHAPTER 17   AN EMPATHETIC CHOKING

by Randy

Well I'm 41 year old gay male. I live in Clinton NC; I work for an Engineer Company. I live in an area that does not deal with gay people the best. (But getting better.) I am in the closet. I'm sure people are starting to suspect. I am kind of shy until you get to know me. I use to be more outgoing but more of a home body now. I am in a relationship. I live out in the country and have lots of animals, chickens, goats, donkeys, cats and a dog. I enjoy the quiet life. I love TV.

Well, I have a small story to share. It happened a year ago. First let me start off, I guess it's weird but I have always had a connection with death and dead people and wanting to know about them and I love cemeteries - it's like I connect with something but not sure what.

But to my story… so last year I awoke around 1:30 AM with this choking feeling. I actually started coughing to get my breath back. Well the next morning I got a phone call that a very good friend of mine had gotten killed in a car accident around 1:30 AM!

His name was also Randy and he was one of the first gay friends I had. We met about 6 years ago. He was very fun to be around - the life of the party. We kind of told each other things that other people didn't know. So we shared that. He introduced me to a lot of gay people which has helped me deal with myself a lot more.

I immediately thought of the choking. I feel that the choking was a way he got in touch with me one last time. I'm really not sure how I feel about it because of the way he died. It makes me feel that he may have suffered a little bit maybe by choking. So that bothers me. He did have a partner and I have never told him about the choking. I may one day.

As far as the cemetery I just love going to them and I feel a presence when I am there - very calming. I usually go walking on my lunch break at a nearby cemetery - it's a big one. It's very peaceful and sometimes I just feel like am being watched over. I am into my genealogy so I visit a lot of old cemeteries where my ancestry is buried. Some are in the woods. But I never get scared.

I collect antiques and I guess this is crazy but I feel that every piece I have connects to the deceased person and that they are all looking out for me in some way. Especially the pieces I have from loved ones.

I did have another friend that committed suicide several years ago. He was my best friend and I did not deal well with it and one night I had a dream that he came to me on the ocean and he hugged me and told me that he was fine and he then jumped into the ocean and came out behind a wave as a beautiful seagull. After that I came to peace with his death.

JOURNEY COMPANION 72

CHAPTER 18   ORGANIZED GROUP OF 12 SPIRITS: DIAGRAM INCLUDED

by Robert L.

I am the youngest of four children from a lower-class Catholic family raised in the western portion of Lansing, Michigan.

I am my mother's baby. All of us kids were unbelievably well-behaved in comparison to how children are encouraged to be high-spirited more recently. Perhaps my mother giving us a redirecting look was a form of intimidation that may seem heavy-handed by today's standards? It is how we were raised and subsequently how the four of us did not step out of line and developed very gentle natures.

My mother and father had us within a five year period and the two oldest are separated by a year simply because my mother miscarried, otherwise there would have been five children which was their plan.

By the time I was born my mother instinctively knew that she was finished having children. It must have been overwhelming to have children so close together.

My parents planned a get-away to Chicago as a well-deserved break on Memorial Day weekend in 1969. They decided to leave the four of us children with different family and friends. I imagine this was an idea not to overburden any particular family with all four of us together. I was just eleven days shy of turning five and this was to be my first time away from both my father and mother.

The family I stayed with was a family who at that point had three boys. The mother was of Jewish decent with lovely thick dark hair and a humorous disposition. The father of the family was of Welsh decent and was towering with auburn hair and I will not be able to remember him fondly. My first night in their house was met with drastic punishment - being whipped with a wet dishtowel - resulting from nervous laughter because the oldest boy had pushed the youngest from the steps resulting in the youngest's tears of protest. The middle boy and I were the recipients of the whipping by the hand of their father as we were seated together in a chair in their living room.

It was an uneasy start to my stay with their family. Early on the Sunday morning of my visit I had to use the bathroom. My intuition kept me in bed as long as possible. I had to break with my intuition and wandered down the hall to the bathroom. When I opened the door to the bathroom the father was standing there waiting for me. He lifted me and carried me down to the first story of their house and then proceeded to carry me into the basement. He set me down and proceeded to force me to perform fellatio on him.

Naturally I could not breathe as he forced his penis in and out of my throat. As he continued I began to feel faint and soon the thought, which is quite foreign to a youngster, came that I might die. Just at that point I realized that I was surrounded by twelve entities that were there to protect me. They assured me telepathically that I would not die and that I was going to be fine.

It is hard to describe an intuitive sensation when its premise is so abstract. I felt them all around me and that circle that enclosed me was composed of twelve and the presence of them was/is unmistakable... Especially when the angels are present. They are VERY POWERFUL!!!

When the father of that family finally finished and ejaculated onto me he began shouting at me explaining that if I were to tell of what happened that he would kill my mother and father. His voice was so loud I thought it would be a matter of moments that someone else in that family would come to my rescue.

But that man terrorized so thoroughly he probably had forced his family into deeper slumbers as he violated my spirit and me. It was due to the guidance of those twelve entities that I found the strength and courage to climb the stairs and continue in to what would become the rest of my life's experience.

Guide

Angel   Angel

Guide   Guide

Angel   Me   Angel

Guide   Guide

Angel   Angel

Guide

It is hard to describe why certain numbers are relevant. I speculate that there is a deep-rooted symbolism why they are separated into what seems like twelve stations. There are so many spiritual concepts that break down into sectors of twelve - for example the Zodiac.

My understanding of how the guides work with me is very sequential. First the guide that is behind me is the higher aspect of myself, the guide in front of me is a mother energy. The guide to the rear right is the guide that assisted me as a child. The guide to the front right is the guide I worked with in young adulthood. The guide in the front left I just began working with several years ago - and beginning work with them was somewhat alarming because it emphasized how I have gone from young adulthood into adulthood! HA! The guide to the rear left will be the guide who helps me in maturity and then to leave this existence.

The angels come when there is alarm and their presence is very remarkable. My Reiki Master felt them arrive during my first Reiki experience and my vision became white and calm.

A few weeks after that molestation experience the thought around it was eating away at me. I knew that I had to be creative about retelling the story because of his threat to kill my mother and father. I explained to my mother that I saw the mother of the family I stayed with naked and that she had a penis. My mother was taken aback and explained that she could not have had a penis, that women do not have penises. I very strongly insisted that she did and that I saw it. My mother curtly responded in disagreement and from her expression that there was not to be another word about this spoken.

Over time the memory was distorted having me open the bathroom door in the opposite direction with a haunting figure that would become completely covered in dark hair, like a Sasquatch. It was not until my twenties that I had recovered enough memory of the event and attempted to seek counseling to be able to process that terrible event. I worked with a number of councilors and was able to recover the full memory thanks to a talented psychotherapist.

During the years of my late twenties, my father noticed that I came to pieces whenever we were with that family. He only had my family visit them twice after my stay with them before he ended his friendship seeing my reactions.

Later in my life that memory kept haunting me until I was just about in my mid to late twenties. I began to deal with that distorted memory and it took me a long time to uncover the real memory. I had a very hard time trying to uncover that memory and I told myself that if only I could get that memory back then everything would be OKAY in my life.

I had many problems as a young man and this problem made me feel worthless. It is how I sank to the point of being so sad that I felt that I could not go on. It took me years to sort through getting back to the real memory of what happened to me that horrible Sunday morning. In fact the psychotherapist I saw that helped me the most was a guy that my ex-partner dragged me to because he was unhappy with our sexual, or lack of sexual, connection. The psychotherapist focused right in on me and realized that my ex-partner was not even to be part of what needed to be worked on. My poor ex-partner got booted from a counseling session that he wanted to have to address our relationship issues!

The psychotherapist performed a technique with his hand that kept my eyes focused on the movement of his hand, but it was not hypnosis, so that my emotions would not become involved and I could go back to the memory of that Sunday morning. It took me two sessions to get back to the memory because it is/was painful. The first session I made it as far as the bathroom door but I could not open it. The second session I opened the door and immediately realized that I was opening the door in the correct direction. No distortion about it at that point. I was able to explain what had happened without even shedding a tear!

In dealing with the effort to recover that difficult memory I was very depressed and sank to a point where I was trying to figure out how to slow down my body enough to attempt to leave this existence. It was during this experience that I was again surrounded by those twelve entities. Again their telepathic assurance was strong and supportive.

I do not see figures or auras. I only feel their presence and communicate with them telepathically but the second experience meeting them was a complete recognition of the same presence that helped me when I was just a young child.

Only because of them, I knew I was not going to die and I was going to be fine. It was from this experience and being older that I knew well enough to hang onto the memory of those twelve entities. I am able to ask them just about anything.

It has been a fun experience for the very most part… I did have a boyfriend once try to lie to me… sort of silly when you have angels that tap into the universe. HA!

There are six guides and six angels. The guides are the ones that communicate to me on a regular basis. It is hard to explain the power of the angels and differentiate them without minimizing the importance of the guides.

Most recently I have been working with a Reiki Master to process past the darkness of that experience. It is such a wonderful and powerful awakening to understand that I am allowed to leave that dark experience behind.

When I was in my mid to late twenties I was under the belief that there could have been a major impact on my sexuality as a result of that traumatic experience. It is no longer my belief that experience impacted my sexuality. I may believe that my level of sensitivity as a gay child could have attracted his capacity to want to impact me negatively. Violating children is in the same vein as shallow hate crimes that take the lives of our brothers and sisters regardless of sexuality. Hate, rage, intolerance - these negative pervasive influences need to be replaced by love.

CHAPTER 19   RADIO AFFIRMS A MESSAGE FROM BEYOND

by Eva Cerezo

I'm a painter from New Zealand, happily married.

I can see why people feel they need to stop you from speaking out about a psychic experience, I guess they don't want people to think that you're crazy or something along those lines, but as you say it never leaves you and you need to share it. People have those visions/premonitions for a reason. They need to be told I think. We people with experiences can lead to healing and comforting those who lost a loved one through a devastating event, whether it is 9/11 or other circumstances. The loss of a loved one is always heartbreaking and we welcome anything that can help us feel they are at peace or in a better place.

I also believe that the right time arrives for things to happen and maybe when we first wanted to speak out about this bizarre happening it wouldn't have been the right moment but now it is. I find comfort in hearing stories like mine because it affirms my belief in spirits and that those we love and have passed look after us and are in a happy place.

Mum has had spiritual encounters on more than one occasion through the years and it's just so interesting to me.

I too have experienced some, two which have stayed with me the most. No premonitions though. I would like to share one of my experiences.

When I was still living at home I had a CD/radio alarm clock which I used to set the alarm on each night to wake me for work. I would select a CD that I wanted to wake up to and set the alarm each night. On weekends I didn't set the alarm as I enjoyed sleeping in a little.

One Saturday morning as I slept my alarm went off loudly and I woke up startled and looked at the CD/alarm clock in confusion. I had not turned the alarm on the night before and it was blaring the 4th track on the CD which was very strange because when the alarm goes off it plays the first track and it goes from there. There was no way I could ever, or have ever, slept through any of the songs, as I am a light sleeper. I couldn't understand how this had happened. It didn't make sense and it really got me thinking so I got up and grabbed the CD cover to see the title of the music which played. The CD was by Guitarist Armik titled *Gypsy Flame* and because it is music with no lyrics I didn't know the title of the track. When I looked at the name of the track my eyes teared up, the music which played was titled – "Meet you in Heaven." I figured it was a message from my grandmother who had just passed and was letting me know that one day we would meet again.

It was very touching and comforting to have received this message.

Last year I read Allison Dubois book titled *We Are Their Heaven*. In this book she mentions how those that have passed can communicate with us by manipulating electrical equipment such as radios, televisions, etc.. This was all the confirmation I needed. I knew now that what I had experienced all those years ago was an electric spiritual phenomenal and confirmed what I had always believed that my grandmother had made contact with me that morning.

Last week when I spoke to my mum she told me that she was going about her house duties and was taken by surprise when she heard music playing - a tune which you normally hear playing from a jewelry box. She followed the sound and it was playing from the lounge room. She moved closer towards the music and realized it was coming from the display cabinet. My mum opened the glass door on the cabinet and the tune was playing from a small gift I gave my mum one year for Mother's Day. It has a heartfelt message dedicated to mums and on the back you wind it up and it plays a tune. My mum picked it up and it stopped playing. A while later she remembered that exactly nine years had passed since her mum had passed away. I told my mum that it must be my grandmother's way of letting her know that she is still watching over her and she is not alone. My mum lit a candle in her memory that day and let it burn all day long, she always places flowers from her garden behind a photo she has in her lounge room of her mum and dad. I thought that was beautiful and very comforting.

My mum has actually experienced the presence of spirits. She has had most encounters when she goes to bed. She will try to turn over but can't because she feels a body beside her when no one is in bed with her and has also been embraced by spirits.

She opens up to me about her experiences because she knows that I believe in spirits. She does get a little frightened when she has these encounters as you can imagine - I would be freaked out even though I know they mean no harm.

CHAPTER 20   RAINY SCOTLAND: ANOTHER COUNTRY & DIMENSION

by Daniel F.

My father died quite suddenly at sixty-one. Our relationship was never good at best. I felt angry because he hadn't been a better father, and guilty because I hadn't been a better son. There didn't seem to be any proper closure.

I decided to get away for a while, and during my travels I visited Stirling, Scotland. With my belly full and map in hand, I began my walk up to the Castle on the hill.

I came to the gates of a building that had been used as a courtroom and prison for centuries. Crimes of blasphemy to murder once tried and sentenced here. Dark shadows watched down at me from behind the black iron bars. Forgotten. Chills ran down my spine.

Beyond the gates and out of the shadows came ten Scottish Pipers playing me a beautiful melancholy serenade. They looked alive but their floating assured these were only solemn spirits summoned back to play the wandering traveler home. Their kilts and hair blew softly in the breeze that whistled through the rolling fog, and empty cobblestone streets.

Memories of my father filled my mind and I was overwhelmed by the sad beauty of the moment. As we approached the top of the hill on the Jail Wynd, I crossed the street as my eyes filled with tears. On the Castle Esplanade, overlooking the top of the hill, the procession ceased. As the pipers formed a circle and continued to play, the sky grew dark, and wind blew wild.

A cold rain began to fall. Rain rolled down their stern faces as they defiantly held their ground while summoning the old gods to take the lost dead home.

The welcoming storm passed quickly. The bright sun moved through the passing clouds warming my face and cold wet clothing. I slowly turned and walked towards the castle gates feeling the moment had come and gone, a miraculous moment, meant only for me.

I departed the train from Inverness in the North West Scottish town of Kyle of Lochalsh. I bought a couple cans of juice from the closest shop, followed the Gulls to the seaside, and boarded the ferry to the Isle of Skye.

As I walked up the hill from the shore, I could see remains of a castle overlooking the ocean surrounded by rugged terrain. A welcoming wave from a driver made me feel at ease and from the expression on his face he looked as if he knew me. I moved to one side of the road to make way for the friendly driver and found myself beside a row of trees beside a tall black iron fence.

Light rain began to fall and a gentle gust of wind eased open the Iron Gate for me! Beyond the gates stood a grand white home surrounded by gardens of enormous white gardenias and lush green grass.

As I wandered the grounds admiring the manicured gardens, my boots had quickly become waterlogged and had begun to squeak with every step. Drops from the sagging trees fell onto my forehead and off the tip of my nose. I brushed my face with the sleeve of my sweater and threw open my umbrella. A violent gust of wind caught hold, turning it inside out. Thick rain began to pour.

I ran out of the gates and back down the path towards an old stone boathouse to take refuge. Kicking away the empty bottles and broken glass, I made a dry place to sit while I waited out the storm. I sat looking out to the fog covered islands in the distance, listening to the rhythmic beat of the rain pounding on the rusted tin roof. Waves crashed violently on the shore, as the storm grew stronger.

I stood with arms in the air and felt the power and strength of the storm surge through me as bursts of spray anointed me through the open door. Everything became silent. The clouds cleared letting the glowing sunlight stream in and onto the old brick wall. A mosaic of brilliant warm color complimented the glowing green grass and shimmering blue sea. There was a still and silent calm as if engulfed in the eye of the storm.

As I ventured out, a blanket of fog, like a ghost, hovered silently around the cabin. I began to walk to the approaching ferry in the distance, and looking back wondered how many travelers before me had taken shelter in this cold enchanted place.

The Newfoundland house I stayed at definitely has some stories as well.

The first time I had stayed there (a couple years ago) I found my bed had appeared to have been slept in - however no one had been there. Shortly afterwards when alone in the kitchen I clearly heard a male voice say "Ah fuck!" with a distinctive Newfoundland rural accent.

The other guests also admitted to hearing voices - and footsteps and someone walking around in the attic. I investigated the attic the next day and there were no signs of animals and not enough head room to actually walk.

There are many photos of ghostly images and orbs outside and around the house that gave me chills

I stayed there alone last September and the mood upstairs was oppressive but I refused to give in to it. I felt as if I was being tolerated. One of the neighbors had stayed the night while her house was being rid of mice. She didn't sleep at all. She felt as if someone was on the bed with her holding her down. Strangely that is the room I feel most comfortable in and have never experienced what she did that night. The land has been occupied for a long time by many including pirates and the original natives who are now extinct as a result of the English and Spanish. I am sure there is lots of dark history on the property because I sense it strongly. Why do I keep going there? It is amazingly beautiful! It seems a spiritual place and my stress fades the moment I arrive. But I wonder just how "out of the world" it is.

I was there a few weeks ago doing some renovations and plan to go back in a few weeks.

CHAPTER 21   BRINGING BOOKS TO A MUTE GIRL IN THE ATTIC

by Doug C.

I was around 12 years old when this dream first occurred. I was dreaming that I, along with a couple of friends or cousins...familiar faces, was trying to find a house that would suit the needs of my family (parents and myself).

We walked into a house that seemed familiar and comfortable and I knew immediately that I had to explore. My friends were not at all interested in doing so...so they left me there to check things out on my own.

I walked through the house and noticed that it was, oddly enough, completely furnished with period pieces. I kept getting the feeling that I had been there before....I recognized some of the furniture (my parents were big collectors of antiques...). The feeling that I had was sometimes comfortable but then would turn to a cold, eerie feeling.

I turned the corner and walked into a dining room where I saw a complete table setting... but it was covered in dust and cobwebs. I looked around the room and noticed a huge mirror over the mantle and as I walked closer to the mirror, I noticed that being reflected were the images of a family having dinner at the table behind me! I spun around and there was no one sitting there. I tried to cry out for my friends but I was too petrified to make a sound.

As I was leaving the room, a little girl came out from behind a door. I was startled at first but then had this feeling of warmth around me...and I knew that she was a good "spirit." I realized that she was mute as she was trying to communicate with me and I noticed a scar on her throat where something had happened to her larynx. She went through the motions of talking to me with her hands and somehow I knew completely what she was trying to convey.

She had a children's storybook that she held out to me and wanted me to read to her. As I read the book to her, I noticed that it was worn and yellowed with age. I asked her if she would like for me to bring her new books and she smiled and shook her head "yes."

As I was leaving, I told her that I would be back tomorrow with new books to read to her. I turned around to say "goodbye"....but she had vanished.

I woke up that morning with a calm that quickly turned to a feeling of dread. It was the strangest thing I had ever experienced. It was more than a dream! I realized the house that I had visited was the same old house that my family and I had been living in for years. The house was built in the early 1900's and is still on the property.

The next night... and I don't know if I had been conditioning myself to revisit this little girl... I had a "dream" that I went back to that house by myself with some new books. I looked around the house for the little girl, but to no avail. Feeling very disappointed and let down, I left the books on the table assuming that she would come and get them.

I had that dream many, many times until my late 20's... and nothing was ever resolved. I often wondered if there was actually someone from a different realm who wanted or needed to communicate with me. Trust me, I made myself open and willing to hear.... and I may have eventually closed that off... I don't know.

After we moved out of that house, my brother and his family, my two nephews and niece, moved in. My niece, Joni, who I've always been very close to, had my old room. A couple of years ago, after they had long since moved out of that house, she asked me if I ever used to hear things in my room, because she did. I told her that I used to see and hear people (or ghosts) all the time.

The pastor at my church (my family is an old German Lutheran family) told me that because I was very artistic (a painter, musician, dancer), I was probably more aware of my surroundings and a bit more sensitive to a 6th sense, even... and that's probably why I had those dreams. He didn't dismiss any idea that something was trying to visit or communicate with me... and he said that some of us are just more fortunate than others.... because we have that sensitivity.

CHAPTER 22   MOTHER-IN-LAW'S VOICE WARNING OF DANGER

by Al W.

I live only 35 miles southwest of New York City, in Green Brook, N.J., and I do take the train to the city every now and again. I usually catch the train from Cranford, NJ to go to NYC but this particular time I used Dunellen Station and the commuter company is called New Jersey Transit.

It's only a one hour ride, much faster if I didn't have to switch trains in Newark. I was planning on going to NYC Sunday, Sept 9th, 2001, to attend an organ concert at St. Patrick's Cathedral. As I was waiting for the train in NJ, I could CLEARLY hear my mother-in-law say to me, "DON'T GO"!!!!"

My mother-In-law passed away from cancer in February of 2000, almost two years before! She was like having another mother, in a positive way, and when she passed away, it was almost as bad as losing my own mother who by the way is still alive. My mother-in-law used to say to me that my treatment of her while she was alive was always as loving as a "GOOD SON." She loved me like a son. Though she had been dead almost two years, it was HER voice and it was crystal clear!!!!! It was profound and I actually listened and didn't go. However, nothing bad happened that day of 09/09/01.

However, less than two days later the World Trade Center was destroyed, along with thousands of innocent victims.

My wife's reaction was, "See that? Mom is helping to take care of us from the other side always watching out for all of us." Then she said to me, "You know my mother really did love you!"

Even 35 miles from the city and let me tell you, two days after 9/11, the winds shifted briefly for about three hours and can you believe that terrible acrid odor from ground zero reached my house???? I thought there was a local fire and I quickly figured out that it was traveling to my town. Unbelievable!!!!!

CHAPTER 23   SECRET LOVE BROKEN: VOICE THAT CAN'T BE SILENCED

by Atticus King

I don't know if you have a face in mind that you could tell me the very first time you saw it, where you were, where he was and the first word or words that person spoke to you - although you'd not actually meet that person for a year and a half. I know such a face. Thirty-eight years later, I could take you to exactly where I was walking, where I stopped. I could place your feet within inches of where his feet were when he said one word.

Eighteen years old, poor, and distraught walking through the student center at a small university in a small Texas City on my way to the stairs that would take me to the registration desk for my freshman year in college. Eighteen and skinny and poorly dressed. Skinny and lonely. Lonely and isolated. Isolated and withdrawn. In my hands were the forms to enroll. In my heart was the sudden realization that walking up those stairs was an option. I could simply bypass them, walk out the door, go back to my belongings, pack them and take a bus home. All around me were people smiling and laughing and talking with friends which emphasized my insignificance. I looked to my left into the cafeteria where I saw many people sharing greetings and bonding. The cafeteria where I could not afford the price of the meal ticket for the semester. A place where the cost of a single meal was cost prohibitive on my survival mode budgeting.

Incapable of continuing that view, I refocused on what lay in front of me, the hallway to the exit. Next is crucial. Next changed every minute of every day of the rest of my life. Next was the beginning of the most incredible joy, the most intense pain, and the basis for whatever success I've experienced in life. Next, I turned my face to realize that I need to move to my right as I was nearing a guy whose simple "Hello" and smile altered my life forever.

In someone's fairy tale, we would have met then. For him then and there my fear and hatred of my sexuality would have fallen away with my discount jeans and shirt as "Heaven on earth" would have acknowledged pure, true and natural love. This is not, however, anyone's fairy tale.

The face that greeted me was a face pale and very lightly freckled. The eyes that looked at me sparkled brilliantly blue in the sunlight glaring through the entrance to the student center. The voice was sincere and warm and enveloping as he walked past me, my breath having temporarily become something I needed to remember to do. I turned to watch him, to see where he was going. It was then that I fell in love with starched white long sleeved shirts, stiffly starched 501s, boots, and platinum hair with a cowlick. And he was skinny! He, however, was clearly not poor. He turned into the cafeteria where there were several friends of his, some wearing blue windbreakers with some sort of lettering on them which meant nothing to me other than that I was not one of them

I'd prefer that you did not think that my thoughts of him at the time were based on sex because, my friend, I'd not had sex with a guy and feared that aspect of my desires. What I'd prefer you see is what happened next. I did not exit the student center; I walked up and registered for my first semester of college because in one fragment of time, a wonderful human being spoke to a stranger and provided him with his first thoughts that he could be a part of this setting, not apart from. I never told him about that; never thanked him for that moment when he gave me the guts to do what was truly best. It was not something he would remember.

It would be over a year before I would see him again.

My freshman year was challenging in ways I could not have anticipated. I was raped by one of my roommates and two of his drunk friends. I could tell no one about that without potentially exposing my true sexuality. My roommate knew that and made my life hell every day after, making fun of me and trying to physically hurt me in other ways to the point that one day when I turned on him we actually fought, and at one point I understood our positioning at the top of a stairway ... and that with just the right push, I could have killed him. I didn't. He stole my textbooks and sold them back at the bookstore. I had no money to replace them. He scribbled filth across the notes in my notebooks so I could not read notes I had taken in classes to study.

I learned places to go to stay away from him as long as I could until I had to sleep. I learned to take baths at odd hours of the day to avoid more abuse. What saved me was his drunken partying in that setting where doing such and having girls involved was not allowed. I came back to college after a weekend at home to find him gone. I barely passed my courses. My success was having survived, as my grades pictured "How much were you partying?"

It may not seem comprehensible to you that I did not report any of this to anyone. What you don't know is that my mother had multiple sclerosis, and she had to believe that I was doing okay. That I was doing well. That I could succeed. I could not be another disappointment in her life. Having been abandoned by her husband when her illness was diagnosed... and having three children to raise on welfare... she succeeded in spite of incredibly overwhelming odds. I could not fail or appear to be a failure in her eyes. For the sake of her health, she could not be confronted with fears of my ability to fend for myself.

Get back to the story, you say.

In the fall of my sophomore year, I had to take a history class late in the afternoon. We were seated alphabetically, which put me next to John, a good looking guy who had a difficult time making it to class on time due to his working hours. I made assumptions. He was poor and badly dressed. I felt sorry for him, and we actually became friends because when he would start to nod off in class, I would nudge him to help him stay awake which he appreciated. When his motorcycle broke down and he did not have the money to repair it, we discovered that we walked in the same direction to go home. His apartment was a matter of only four blocks from mine.

I should add that Pat was one of those guys whose looks inspired girls to stop dead in their tracks and their breasts to swell at the thought of his touch. He seldom had to take many steps before a car would stop to give him a ride which often helped me in the process. One evening he asked me if I wanted to come in for a beer. I accepted.

No big deal, you say. I say that nothing could be further from the truth. You see, he got me a beer, left me in the living room, and went to the bathroom to take a shower. I sat. On the coffee table in front of me was a magazine. It was called Phi Illustrated, a Phi Delta Theta recruiting magazine published by the fraternity to recruit new members. On the cover, yes, on the cover was John's picture. John playing football. I could not believe what I was seeing as I flipped through the pages until I found the article about him. President of the sophomore class and Phi Delta Theta, not at all the poor guy with whom I'd empathized. In my own "out-of-it-ness" I had had no clue that this person, my friend John, was one of those guys who had one of those blue windbreakers with the Greek letters. He had a life I knew nothing of other than that I had no money to be a part of it. I could not bring myself to tell him that I had had no clue who he really was.

In the spring semester of that school year, he moved into my apartment because he could afford it better and because I was someone who'd help keep him on track with school. Before you take this story into the avenue of self-revelation and sexual experience, I'll stop you. Yes, later after he had transferred to the University of Texas to live with his hippie freak, druggy girlfriend and himself became someone who'd be arrested for selling pot, he did become someone I would tell that I was gay. He wrote back to say that he appreciated the honesty and shared that he was having trouble with drugs but was not gay. But that is another story not with much relevance other than satisfying your curiosity or adding clarification.

What matters is what he returned to my life.

One hot and sweaty east Texas afternoon nearing the end of the spring semester, I sat by the open window studying and wishing for air conditioning. I heard two sets of footsteps coming up the wooden stairs. I looked up as two people came into my bedroom. One was John. A hand was extended in front of my face, a hand attached to pale, vaguely freckled arm. I looked up to hear, "Hi, I'm Horace Wardlow. It is nice to meet you. John talks about you a lot." Those blue eyes sparkled. The platinum hair shone. And the smile enveloped me. My hand was in his hand. It was May of 1969, and he had had a rough afternoon digging post holes on his father's property for fencing for their Arabian horses... "You see, my dad gave me the Firebird for graduation, but he said if I want to have a motorcycle like John's I have to earn the money and buy it for myself. He and mom don't want me to have one."

We were in college and Horace was a very popular fraternity boy who still lived at home with his parents and one of his two brothers. He was also still working when he could for his father to buy that motorcycle...

… which he died on the day he got it which I left out of the story.

There was an upcoming Arabian horse show, and he was excited about that too because they'd flown in some new ones from Arizona to show. I did not see him that day. I was living in an apartment, but I could not afford it alone, so between our very different courses of study and his working and involvement with the fraternity that I could not be a part of, and his still living at home, it is not as if we had the living together kind of time that would have been a dream come true in the world of 1970 ... or gotten us killed. A huge portion of my regret from that time period is the contrast between frequency of time together and length of time together and what people picture today as being lovers. In its time frame and reference though, it was truly special ... for fourteen months. He died before we could have experienced the freedom to have more. That is a portion of my difficulty in writing about it.

He died July 28, 1970 at 6:40 PM. Two blocks from home on a drizzly evening, on that motorcycle, he swerved to avoid hitting a tiny puppy that ran in front of him. The puppy lived. He lost control of the motorcycle, and helmet or not, necks break when they encounter telephone poles and an arm can be nearly severed by the fender of a motorcycle flipping and landing on you.

Sitting on my bed, again studying as I was in summer school taking French and International Government, I cannot tell you what song was in the background on the radio when it was interrupted with the statement, "We have just learned that a 21 year old university student has been killed in a motorcycle accident. He was pronounced DOA upon arrival at the hospital. The name is being withheld until all of his family has been notified." My heart sank into overwhelming tears, an oblivion of anger. I knew. This man whom I loved was now and forever apart from my life. I sat there, lost in vacant listening to that station because there was no life without hearing it actually said. Finally, it was said.

With that knowledge I needed somewhere to be. And I walked to his church, his church that kept its doors open all night for those who needed to pray. I went there because there I could cry and pray and be in the church that had been his church all of his life. No one could tell me that I did not belong. Perhaps, there I would not need to die. I would fail a test in government. At that moment in my life no government mattered. For what reason did another breath matter? I had walked twenty minutes to his church, not once having truly felt the ground under my feet that I could recall or having seen an existing human being.

Later in life, recalling that time frame, I wrote, "Through this veiled gray cloud I cannot see." It was, at that time, the clearest I can explain the wanderings of my body and my soul as I lived in the mist of memory, gray, physical and emotional withdrawal, and death. No one would understand; there was a new silence my soul knew as I knew a funeral was coming, one in which I would play no role other than spectator sitting in the back apart from his family as six fraternity brothers would carry him in ... and out to be placed in the earth. I would put on my suit and walk in to his church knowing that I could not cry, and the walk to the cemetery would take me about forty-five minutes, and the July heat and humidity would make me look like the outsider that, to his family, I indeed was.

To my surprise after I sat down in one of the few remaining spaces available, only seconds passed before I heard a familiar voice, looked up, and there was John who'd driven from Austin for the funeral. I had a ride to the cemetery. It was something of consolation to me that once again John was seated next to me, John who cried as he told me that he knew that he was not as welcome as he once would have been had he not moved to Austin and joined in the Peace movement.

"I don't know," he said, "What they've told you about me and things, but I want you to know that some of what I've heard is being said is not true."

He was lying. It was true and he was only months away from prison. You see; it was after that, and a night of heavy drinking, that I wrote him of truth, partial truth in order to gauge how much truth he could handle and to learn how much trust I could place in him to learn more. Sober, I regretted that trip to the mailbox to try and find someone with whom I could share the hollowness of my existence, someone who'd respond by telling me that he loved me, that he understood. Two weeks later, I got that letter which shared more truth of his life, questioned nothing of mine, and told me to be very careful about sharing such a "hated" thing with others.

He did not tell me that he loved me. He did not reference with a single word the death or the desire to continue correspondence with me. He did mention, however, fraternity brothers with whom he was still in contact. I knew, without the words, words I would never say to him.

I was at a doorway, one that cannot be seen but can be felt. An exit without the sign. It can be difficult to open a door when you cannot see the knob. You see, I was failing my courses. I was nearly flat broke and had several weeks ahead before the next installment of my student loan and grant would arrive. I would have to choose between writing a hot check and being hungry. I could go to the bank and ask my uncle for a loan and hear him call me a failure one more time. My uncle, who could have introduced me to Horace in the fall of my freshman year since he knew that family, was employed in their bank. My uncle who was too ashamed of his poor nephew to do such a thing. I could take my mentally and emotionally devastated body on a long walk to the bank to hear that. I could hear him tell me no. I could go home having failed my courses skinnier than I had been three years before. I could be an embarrassment to my mother.

I found the knob in late August. After nightly walks to the cemetery and sitting by his grave and talking and crying and burying a silver pinky ring that I wore to symbolize him in my life where I approximated his heart was, I knew where the knob was. I knew happiness. I could smile. The knob was in a drawer by my mother's bedside, heavy duty pain killers of a couple of varieties. A couple of weekend trips home, a little theft, and I could open the door, the exit, the entrance where I'd perhaps find a particular face to say, "Hi, I'm Horace Mast." A far better thing, and safer than sitting by a grave at night feeling the enormity of singularity.

You may be asking if I did not fear Hell as a consequence of such an act. No. The "logic" that coursed my thoughts was that I was in Hell, and I was the source of pain to others who'd be far better off without me and learning more of who I was. If I turned the knob, yes, I might find Hell on the other side... and Hell without Horace. What needed to end, however, was a pain stronger than my body, a pain that shredded thought. Turning the knob would bring relief for everyone. They'd eventually understand. And who were they anyway as they did not fill this void? These people with whom I could not share my soul?

I don't know that that will make sense to you. For your sake, I hope not. Putting those feelings into words is an exercise in being handicapped, feeble. Words can't touch that level of despair and logic that is not logical at all.

You, at this point, do not believe that I turned the knob. After all, you are reading this truth. And the truth is that I turned the knob. I took from my mother's drawer some of the relief for her pain. I took it back to the university with me. I made a trip to the cemetery to share my plans for an entrance into his new existence, went home ... and with a glass of warm water swallowed, turned the knob.

It did not open.

My next reality was sixteen hours later when I woke up and could not hear. And I cried. I had failed, and the knob was all gone. Not only had I failed, I could now not hear. I was hungry, and there was little to eat. I was alive but dead to the world, a world that did not need or want me in it. My failure as a human had now been elevated to a new and embarrassing new height. I could not even successfully end my own existence. There was only one place to go, or two, or three.

A cemetery and a church in the darkness of night. A hard and dark trip to the cemetery, and sharing of another failure sitting by a grave and filtering the dirt through my fingers. Going to classes was a thought, and I did go only because it was somewhere to be surrounded by people. Lacking the ability to read lips, however, it was an exercise in futility. My hearing was returning bit by bit so my fears of continued existence deaf were diminishing. Starvation, however, was around the corner.

There was no money for a bus ticket back to my mother's bedside drawer. I had to live. At least for a little while longer in order to be able to find that knob again and ensure success. I needed to pass the courses in order to get my check for the next semester.

A few days later when my hearing had returned to normal, I put my feet to the task of walking to the bank, to humiliate myself and pray that my uncle would, through the bank not his own money, loan me enough money to be able to eat. After all, I had paid them back once before. I did have some credit rating going on. Every fear of words I'd had proved to be minuscule in contrast to the things he said to me about what a true embarrassment I'd grown into, how he was ashamed to have to admit being related to me, a twenty-one year old man who still called his mother, "Mommy." He continued, "You used to be able to take part of your college grant money and send it home to your mother. You used to have a way to even buy clothes for your sister. What the Hell have you done with your life?" "Are you a man," he asked to conclude his sermonette on his own mountain. Finally, he agreed that the bank would loan me a hundred dollars only because he could not give a loan for less. His final wording was that he never wanted to look up and see me in "his" bank for everyone there to see his failure of a nephew wanting a handout again. In the swirl of negativity that my mind was, he added a new level to my capacity for hatred. He added to my need to relocate the knob to the only door where relief waited on the other side.

You ask, "What did you say to all that?" Surely you know me by now. I said nothing. How could I have said, "When I had the money to send, I had no life outside of going to and from class and trying to avoid being abused again. I am having a rough time because I found a life, a love, but he died." You cannot reasonably believe I could say those things. I would be able to eat. I would be able to plan better.

Days passed, a week. There was a call. "Your grandmother is in town. She wants to see you." So, I walked to my uncle's home and there she was waiting.

Before you get excited and think that this would be the heartwarming moment, my salvation, there's a story within this story. A flashback if you will. I'm five years old and a rowdy little kid who loves to be a cowboy and a fireman and drive a train because five year-olds can do anything for careers in spite of what tall people say. I was rowdy and loud and outspoken. What I did not comprehend were our new circumstances. My mother could no longer walk without a cane. Within two years she would be in a wheelchair. I did not understand that our financial status had changed from upper middle class to applying for welfare. What I understood was that there were lives to be saved and no one could attack me if I were in the Mimosa tree where the title King somehow blended with my firefighting, train driving, and being a true cowboy. I had my little red fire truck I could pedal around the yard. I had my machine gun and my pistol. I knew who I was, and I had power. I was the kid who could walk by the photographer's studio and see my picture enlarged beyond life size in the window as a sample of the work. I was the kid in the family who had blue eyes and platinum blonde hair. I was the winner.

One afternoon after a particularly exciting day of saving lives, I ran up the steps, opened the screen door and let it slam behind me. I suppose I must have been told that I had to be a quieter child since my mother's nerves were now very fragile. I must have been told that sudden noises could cause her pain. I must not have understood or I forgot in the heat of my excitement. My grandmother was at the house visiting her daughter.

She grabbed my wrist before I got to the hallway and led me to my bedroom and put me on the corner of my bed with its cowboys and horses bedspread. She said, "If you are a bad boy, you are going to kill your mother. And you are a bad boy. If your mother dies, you will have to go live in an orphanage, and you will be there until you are eighteen years old because you are bad and no one will ever love or want you."

Those, my friend, are words that sear your heart and embed themselves in the depths of your brain …. until death.

She was scared. She wanted her daughter to live and be healthy, and she - no – you need the truth. She had actually sought out families to adopt the three little kids we were because our mother was incapable of caring for us. Grandmother had found families to take my older brother and my baby sister, but she had not been able to find a family to take me. She and my two uncles had tried to talk my mother into putting us up for adoption because they sincerely believed our mother would live longer without the burden of us. She, being the true definition of a mother, refused. Her statement to me was angered and part of what she said was a frustrating truth. She could not find someone to take me.

Ask me when I slammed the door again. Ask me when I next climbed my tree fortress. Ask me when I knew I was king and mattered. Or don't. You know the answers. I found the storeroom in the garage where I would not be leaving the yard or slamming a door, and I could pretend there were people who could love me. There I could not do a bad thing, and I would not kill my mother. Who I had been I would never be again. What I knew best was fear. During the next few years, I decided that I was adopted and preferred to be outside my grandparents' house when we had Sunday visits there for lunch after church because, after all, I was not one of them. There was a family somewhere that I really belonged with, but they had not wanted me either.

Now you have some clarity which will make what happens next in the big story more easily understood both in what was said and the level of its impact.

It was summer. It was hot. I had gone to classes wearing a Tee-shirt and cut-off jeans for shorts. My feet were bare. It was 1970 and there were hippies and free love and a war going on that my draft status and then lottery number kept me away from. There were things that mattered in the world, and Horace was dead. I could hear; I could eat; I could plan. I honored the demand that I go there. Part of me thought it would be okay. After all, I'd get to eat a meal probably and a better one than I'd fix.

That would have been nice. You are trying to picture that, right?

Picture this instead. I'm walking up the brick driveway. The door opens. There grandmother is coming short and squattily toward me, no smile of greeting. "Don't tell me that you went to school looking like that! Are you trying to embarrass your whole family? You won't be coming in this house with those dirty feet!"

I turned and walked away. I'd heard worse. "You are bad …. No one will ever want or love you." I suppose a part of me thanked her for the reminder as she added to my resolve to truly resolve the situation in my favor. Part of me could see her at my funeral pretending to cry. No part of me pictured regret other than the cost of a box and some flowers.

You want to take a guess about what happened next? If I told you that I had the money to buy a really large bottle of aspirin, would you be very surprised? You would be comforted, I suppose, to know that I quite obviously failed again.

That is not what happened though.

I went to church, prayed to die. When darkness fell, I returned to that piece of ground now holy to me. I sat and talked into the air of love and loss and worthlessness. I talked about happiness in being loved and loving so much in return. I asked if Horace and I'd be able to feel each other again when reunited. I fingered the ground searching to see if it would find the ring, and pushed it deeper so that no one would ever find it and learn what was none of their business. I promised the air that I was to become a part of it and of him. Nothing would alter the life after life I so desperately needed. Someone really could love me.

The lecture you are tempted to make about my mother, etc.. Don't go there. There's a level of hollow that some people experience as others cannot possibly comprehend. What my grandmother and no one else who saw me during that time understood was that basically all that was left of a person they knew was that shell that moved him.

That shell got up, walked in the late, late night hours back to the apartment to experience another night of alone. Beyond tears. There was a plan and a reason to smile. Beyond this pain there could again be love and laughter and forever. Those, my friend, are the thoughts that take you to sleep. There is the chance, you know, that you won't have to wake up.

Picture all-encompassing blackness. Make it darker though. Darker than night. Picture yourself weightless, engulfed in a blackness that feels like air but thinner. Don't think you can see yourself either because there is nothing whatsoever to see. It is not day. It is not night. It just is. There is no element of time. Close your eyes; see if you can get there.

Somewhere in that night, in that sleep, that universal, calm darkness surrounded me. No sound. No movement. No breathing. In that darkness I was suddenly embraced through to my soul by arms I could not see as all I knew was love. No fear, no confusion, no question. An embrace unlike anything I'd ever felt as the warmth and strength of it surpassed the capacity of a human to fill another's being with a different "warm." And his voice. From the nowhereness of this enveloping blackness, very clearly, Horace said, "Atticus, it's okay. It's really okay." The depth of the embrace increased, and as suddenly as it happened it was gone. And the voice.

I "woke up" from the ":dream" warmer inside than out. I could still feel the "pressure" of the hug around my chest and back. Horace Wardlow had reached out to me from beyond to save my life.

I was not given a dream.

I was provided a moment of Heaven.

That beautiful young man whose smile and "Hello" had gotten me up frightening stairs to enroll in college had now saved my life. I know what it is to be loved. He is and was my timekeeper, the meaning of the name Horace.

Can I prove any of that? Do I have pictures or a recording? How do you prove happiness? How do you record feeling?

What happened defies logic. One could reason this or that as causes of the warm feeling and the hug as a tight blanket. There was no blanket. I had not bothered to get under any cover. Actually, my own mind took me later into more questions than you can possibly have. What I had to grip was faith in what had truly happened. Just as the love that existed happened without the knowledge or consent of others, a feeling very private for two people, a feeling no one can see or feel… this had happened in its own significantly private way. It was not significant that anyone else sees or feels it. I hope you choose to believe.

"Atticus, it's okay. It's really okay."

If I could, I'd give you that darkness and a feeling beyond compare. I'd not wish you the road that led there.

"Atticus, it's okay. It's really okay."

Whom did I tell? No one. There was no one to tell who'd care to listen given the background information that would startle them first followed by a story of an awakening from Heaven. Perhaps even more significant was that this was mine, mine! Strength to overcome was mine. That mattered more.

The following spring I did my student teaching, American government. Seated four seats from the front on the second row from my left was a frail, blonde boy with more cowlicks than a pasture and an impish grin on his Howdy Doody face. His name… John Wardlow. Horace's younger brother whom I had never met. I had, in fact, only seen him once… at a funeral. He knew nothing of me. There was a "goodness" and an innocence which lay waste to any consideration of sharing with him things which might hurt him. There would be no telling him about a hug.

For nine short weeks, forty-five fifty minute periods I would see him, and occasionally we talked.

One morning as my students were taking a test, I was walking up and down the aisles monitoring them for, yes, cheating and for nearness of completion. I stopped at his desk noticing that his senior ring was different from everyone else's. He looked up, saw me looking at it. Without a word, he took it off and held it out to me. "It was my brother's," he said.

I took off the college senior ring which I wore, could afford only because of a drawing for a free one, and handed it to him. I put on Horace's high school senior ring. It was a perfect fit.

For an instant, I once again felt the completeness of a hug and a reconnection beyond physical. Some moments, however, are tempered by reality. Reality was that I was wearing a student's ring in a classroom, and I had to take it off in a realistic time frame to avoid any appearance of impropriety. I gave it back.

What inspired him to do that? I never asked. I knew.

For those brief seconds, three people who shared love were connected through John's sharing. Later in life, John would have a son, and he would give him his brother's name. That son would major in engineering and, ironically, love speed and work on the development of high performance engines. That Horace has now lived three years longer than the man for whom he is named.

As I write this, I cannot help but recall that next month, the 25th day of it, will be the 59th anniversary of the birth of my Horace. A truly good man who lived twenty one years, three months, and three days. A man who loves me. You see, even at fifty-nine, I still have moments of feeling too alone. I get mad at Christmas sometimes … and Valentine's Day too. And many times more than once, when my mind is traveling down the "poor little pitiful me" road jealous of those people in those commercials where everyone is always happier with this or that object being peddled for the economy and my heart has drooped with some negative thoughts …. well, they've been interrupted by a voice saying, "I've loved you every day."

Is there something that could matter more?

Believe me.

You see, today at work and during my lunch I decided to research the existing Horace and see what has happened with him in the about two years since the last time I took that adventure. Don't google without a shield! When I typed in his name and Nacogdoches, Texas the item at the top of the list was not about him. It was a page dedicated to those of the 1967 graduating class of Nacogdoches High School who had died, a page that was posted as part of the 40th reunion... I guess. There is a picture of Horace there... 17... and smiling... and beside it, word for word, directly from a newspaper... his obituary. Never ever in my life did I think I'd be reading those words again or that the resulting feeling after all these years could feel like a brand new beating.

NOTE to the reader from Thom Bierdz:

I had started collecting accounts for this book over ten years ago, but did not complete this until 2019 (because after 30 years of rejections from literary agents and publishers, I learned how to self-publish [consequently this is just one of ten ripened books I will have out within a twelve month period]). Anyway, preparing this final edit and reviewing this chapter ten years or more after initially receiving it, like you, I am once again floored at Atticus King's brilliant writing and vulnerability. But I have no recall of our exchanges or how I knew him or how he sent me this chapter.

Was he a fan of my soap opera character and one of my 10,000 Facebook friends? I cannot find him on FB. I do not have his email.

I Googled "Atticus King" expecting to find a mature gay man and award-winning author - but only a young Filipino billionaire pops up – certainly not the same Atticus King. Googling "author Atticus King" I did find one gay mystery novel from 1996 titled *PRETENSE OF INNOCENCE*.

Atticus – If you are out there, please let us know how your life is at this point. You are one of the most captivating and gifted writers I have ever experienced. Thank you for sharing your gripping story. We want to read more!

CHAPTER 24   READING MY MIND BENEATH A TEMPLE IN THAILAND

by John L.

Thom, your 9/11 story is totally believable. Years ago, I would have said like many others you were a nut case, but in retrospect, I have come to realize that there is definitely someone somewhere watching over me, and that there are things which are very hard to rationally explain.

I'm an endurance windsurfer, and years ago was lost 12 miles out at sea, from Key West, in a very bad storm with winds up to 60 mph. My equipment broke apart in the high winds, and I had to swim and float for nearly 6 hours in the cold water. The Coast Guard refused to even go out and look for me because they said at my age, I was already dead for sure, and the storm was bad. I made it through. Nothing psychic here, but I know Someone was beside me during this long ordeal.

I have only two incidents of "unexplained" occurrences, both very dramatic, and lacking in logical explanation.

A friend pushed me into seeing a psychic. I sat there silently, refusing to tell her anything that might give her a clue. I sat with my arms folded, and apparently a "so show me what you have" look on my face. Finally she said, "Stop blocking me." I looked amused, and relaxed as she told me of incidents in my past that no one else knew. I was to visit her many times until we became friends, then as if a switch had been pulled she could no longer read me with the accuracy she had when we were "strangers."

I was only to see one more psychic. How is this for strange? I was on a tour of the Royal Palace in Bangkok. We had a small van and I was on the tour with two adults from India and their four screaming bratty kids. The tour guide took all he could, and announced a 45 minute "free time" where the family could shop for souvenirs. He then pulled me aside and apologized profusely.

He then hit me with a totally unexpected offer. We went into the Buddhist Temple there, and I told him if I was associated with any religion at all, it would be Buddhism. He then told me he was a divinity student in the gigantic underground facility under the temple. He asked if I would like to meet his mentor, which I of course said yes.

We went down into the depths of the underground school, and he introduced me to an ancient man, whom looked as if he was 100+ years old. That is until I saw his eyes which sparkled like rare gems. He took my hand and looked into my eyes intently for a time, and slowly began a dialog in Thai (he spoke no English). The young Buddhist student translated.

The man asked if I knew why I was so attracted to Thailand, where I had traveled a few times. I said I liked the demeanor of the people and felt very comfortable with them. He gave me an all knowing glance and a wink, because at the time I was thinking how I loved the Thai men with their broad shoulders and wasp waists. I do truly love the country and lifestyle as well. He told me I was an Asian in another lifetime, and that I still have very strong Asian traits, such as discipline, control, etc.. I smiled, not really believing. I asked him what I did in the other life, to which he replied, "You were just a normal man with a normal life."

He must have sensed that I didn't believe him, so he changed course, and began to tell me of all the traumatic events in my life that had combined to mold my persona. What a revelation!! Not only did he know intimate details of my entire life, both very good, very bad, and in between, but was then able to show me how to live more comfortably with myself. He told me of incidents as an infant and small child, which I had absolutely no knowledge. I was later able to confirm some of them with older (shocked) relatives, to the extent that I realized everything he told me was true. I never did tell my relatives how I knew what had gone on. I have been a different person ever since, substantially happier, just understanding how I was composed as a man.

We ended up there for over an hour, and I left having the greatest spiritual experience of my life. Here was a man whom knew nothing of me, didn't speak my language, yet knew more about me than I did myself. It was as if he had been walking by my side all my life, taking notes. He would take no money, so instead, I left a donation upstairs in the temple as we left. It was the most positive and enlightening hour of my life.

CHAPTER 25   SPIRIT GUIDES EXPLAINED & EERIE CRIMINAL BOND

by Wayne

I'm 56, soon to be 57. Popular? I have lots of friends and I have the ability to put people at ease. I'm practical, down to earth, but friendly with a good sense of humor.

I'm single, my home town is Odessa, Texas. I believe I'm middle class. I live in a three bedroom house - a real fixer-upper that I've been remodeling for years.

I have brown hair (with highlights of course) and brown eyes.

I was a social worker for 30 years working with the aged and disabled, protecting people who are abused, neglected, or financially exploited and that has been my passion. It's always been a privilege to help people in need. I was a supervisor in this field for 26 years.

I've been psychic all my life. When I was three years old I suddenly recalled having lived three prior lives. It was years before I understood it but I instinctively knew I couldn't discuss this with my family, so I kept it to myself well into my adulthood.

My path led me into astrology, reincarnation, hypnosis, Native American spirituality, religion, psychic development, spirit guides, auras, tarot, etc.. I worked as a psychic in psychic fairs for five years.

My first gift is clairvoyance, the ability to "see" psychically. I can see auras which also allows me to see past lives.

Clairaudience - the ability to hear voices - is my second psychic gift, so I can communicate with both my spirit guides as well as people who have crossed over.

I learned about the four psychic gifts by studying with a group who call themselves "The Inner

Peace Movement." Sounds like a cult but it's not. It's a group who teach psychic development and I learned a lot from them. They don't seem to be as active anymore.

My "hearing" is so good that when I was in acappella choir in high school I could practice my part at home because I could "hear" the others singing in my head. Kind of like replaying a tape in my head. It wasn't until I got to be an adult that I realized I could actually talk with my guides.

The first time I heard voices, I was about 11 and was riding my bicycle behind an L-shaped shopping center. I rode there a lot because it was a big wide open area. After being there a while I decided to go home. I took off and was about to round a corner when I heard these voices yell at me: "Stop. A car is coming!" It shocked me so much I stopped just in time to avoid being hit by a car driving fast into that space. Saved my life! It startled me but I couldn't figure out who or what the voices were and decided to ignore it.

Years later when I was 19 I had moved to San Angelo, Texas to finish college. San Angelo has a river downtown as well as a few lakes on the outskirts of town.

My twin sister and I had moved there so I could finish school and so she could get away from our mother. My niece, who is about six years my junior, would come down for the weekend with a friend.

Once we were out at the lake all day. At that period I couldn't swim very well - all I could do was dog-paddle. So I would lay on my air mattress, then get off and swim a little, etc..

After several hours of that someone suggested we go make a picnic and take it to the Concho River in town, so we did.

After we got there I had a notion that I wanted to swim to the other bank, so I got in the water. I didn't realize how tired my arms were, so halfway across I went under. I managed to get above the water again to take a big gulp of air, then went under again. My arms just wouldn't work anymore.

In panic situations I get very calm. I was depressed at that point of my life because I was gay and didn't know what to do about it. I didn't want to be different but couldn't change my nature. So when death presented itself to me I was ready for it. I thought to myself, "This will be easy. All I have to do is just breathe in and it'll all be over."

I fully intended to do it when the voices yelled at me again: "You can't die now. You have to at least try. We promise it'll get better."

I was startled. When you're under water you don't expect a group of people to yell at you. They showed me what to do since I couldn't get above water on my own: they showed me I could crawl along the bottom of the river. Suddenly I emerged on the other bank and flopped onto the ground like a dead fish. I was amazed. I'd never heard of anyone doing it that way before.

My family and friend were hysterical because they saw me go under. One of them had jumped in the water to try to rescue me and the other two jumped in the car and drove around. They were screaming and crying and carrying on. While that was going on I kept thinking, "Who were the voices?"

I didn't discuss it with them at the time because I knew they wouldn't understand.

Heck I didn't understand it was my guides until years later. I've sure had a strange life.

By the way, it occurs to me I need to explain a little about our guides.

Before we're born into a life on Earth we make contracts with certain people (spirits) who become our guides. They are specially trained because when we're in Heaven for a while we forget how difficult it is to live down here.

In Heaven there is no negativity, no hunger, no pain, no discomfort, no difficulty. These guides are trained to remember these things so they can help those of us who need their services. Together we make an outline of events we want to experience here on Earth. In no way do we plan for everything but we do plan on meeting certain people at various points in the upcoming life.

We may decide we want to work on certain traits and talents we developed in previous lifetimes. For example, Thom, you wanted to work on your acting and art skills. You also wanted to work on your psychic abilities.

Our guides whisper things in our ears from time to time which help us to make decisions that are part of our plan. They use the voice in our head that we all have, so we think it's us thinking those ideas. We have free will so we are free to act upon those ideas... or not.

We also usually plan on five exit points in our lives. These are places where we have the opportunity to die if things we came to learn aren't working out. By the way accidents do happen so we can die at a point we didn't plan for but usually our guides will try to get our attention and divert us from those accidents. Accidental death occurs when we ignore their warnings. This is rare, though. Most deaths that occur are one of the five exit points.

We will also contract with others in Heaven who are about to be born on earth if it's a significant relationship (good or bad) that we want to experience together.

Our guides will make suggestions during the planning phase and we're free to agree or reject what they suggest.

For this reason people we know here on Earth who die do not become our guides. That's not allowed because they haven't been trained. They can, however, stay with us and make contact from the spirit world (Heaven).

We may serve as spirit guides for others when we're in Heaven after going through the training.

This next is sort of two stories in one. It's a long one but you'll want to read it all in one setting.

When I was 25 I'd just started working for the state as a caseworker in the Aged and Disabled division. I moved into a small apartment near the hospital in Odessa. It was late March and it was a nice, warm Spring Saturday. I'd just returned from shopping.

I decided to take a nap so I raised the window in the living room, then I went into my bedroom and closed the living room door and the door to the bathroom to make it dark. I sleep better when it's completely dark.

I normally sleep in my underwear so as I removed my shirt and my outer shorts, something told me to put my clothes within reach of the bed. This wasn't normally my custom but I didn't question it. I was later glad I did.

I'd just dozed off when I heard loud pounding on my front door. It startled me and made me angry that someone would knock so rudely, so I decided to remain in bed. The knocking ceased and I returned to sleep.

What had to be moments later my bedroom door opened. I looked up and saw a young man standing there and I thought I was surely dreaming. I asked, "who are you?" and he shushed me. I still believed I was dreaming because none of it made sense. My logical mind kept insisting I was awake so I decided this guy was running from someone.

The man (I later learned was 19) was breathing hard as if he'd been running. He removed his shirt and opened my bathroom door. Even with both doors open I had difficulty seeing clearly because it was still somewhat dark in my bedroom - but I could see he had something that looked like a knife. I later learned it was a Phillips screwdriver that he'd taken out of one of my kitchen drawers. There were all sorts of knives in there he could have taken - to this day I wonder why he grabbed a screwdriver. But that just figures. I can't even die in a normal way.

At any rate he was pacing between my bathroom, my bedroom, and the living room. I couldn't help but notice he had an erection the whole time he was there which was a bit disconcerting. Since I had a sheet over the lower half of my body I can only assume he thought I was naked. I definitely wasn't in the mood to have sex with a stranger in my apartment, especially one carrying a Phillips screwdriver.

Suddenly there was furious pounding on my front door again. "Graham, we know you're in there." "I know he's in there, I saw him climb in the window." "Do you think we'll have a shootout?"

"Oh my God," I thought to myself. Looking back I realize how silly I was: the biggest fear I had was that someone would fire a bullet into my king-sized water bed, thereby ruining it.

The gears in my mind were running full tilt and I was super alert. I get dead calm in situations that make others panic. I have no idea why I do it, but I'm grateful for it. I knew I was going to get out of this situation safely but had to be alert to any opportunity.

The cops kept pounding on the door. "Kick it in, dammit," I said to myself. "What's wrong with them?"

Graham emerged from the bathroom again. I asked him if the police were in the alley and he said "No." "It looks like you could crawl through the window and escape," I suggested.

Instead he asked, "Where's your car?"

I didn't know what to think. Like we were going to walk calmly through the crowd of officers for us to go get my car. I lied: "It's in the shop." I realized I wasn't dealing with a super-intelligent fellow.

It occurred to me I could do a better job of being a cop or a crook than these people. In the meantime the cops kept pounding on the door and talking amongst themselves. I'm sure this was good entertainment to my neighbors who were, no doubt, also wondering why this was taking such a long time to unfold.

At one point when Graham went into the living room, I grabbed my shorts and put them on under the sheet. I decided if I was going to have company I needed to at least be halfway dressed. The cops kept pounding on the door and I kept trying to send them mental thoughts about kicking it in... they didn't get it.

I decided I was going to have to take action since no one was doing anything differently - I was rapidly getting tired of the situation and wanted everyone to leave.

At one point Graham came into my bedroom and looked through my wallet on the dresser. When I saw him pick up my wristwatch, the watch I'd paid $200 for, I knew he wasn't leaving my apartment with it. That really made me angry. $200 was a lot of money to me in those days.

I got my wish. Suddenly Graham came into my bedroom and did something completely unexpected. He climbed over me into bed! In that split second I thought, "Are you nuts?"

Be that as it may, I knew I had my opportunity. I jumped out of bed because I knew I had to go open the damned front door for the oh-so-polite police officers. As I got up Graham tried to grab me, still clutching his screwdriver. I knew he didn't realize it was a sloshy water bed. As he lunged for me a big wave came up and moved him away from me towards the wall. "Idiot."

I walked into the living room and was startled to see a cop kneeling by the front door, aiming a revolver at me. Some stroke of genius caused them to shift their focus from my front door to the window which was only inches away. It took them 30 minutes to notice it, but I have to give them credit for their creativity.

In his haste Graham forgot to lock my window after he crawled through it. I'm sure the window screen propped up against the outside of my apartment was a clue if one stopped to dwell upon it. One crafty police officer finally noticed it and decided to see if he could raise it, and to his surprise it worked. He climbed inside with the intent of unlocking the front door when a man came running out of the bedroom - that was me.

As the cop and I stared at each other, we realized we knew each other: we graduated in the same high school class. Bill unlocked the front door and they ran into my bedroom to get Graham.

One of the cops instructed me to come down to the police station later to give a statement and to get my watch back.

After they left, a married couple who were friends of mine showed up just in time to see the tail end of what had just transpired. As they walked into my apartment with their mouths agape, the phone rang. It was my older sister, Frances, who worked as a secretary for the Odessa Police Department.

I told her that someone named Graham Davisell, aka Graham Pilobles, had just been carted off by the police, and I told her the story while Doris and Fernie listened - still with their mouths open.

After I finished telling my story, Frances told me she knew Graham very well, both at the police department and at the Ector County Coliseum. Frances had been working part-time at the Coliseum and had talked me into doing the same. I began working there a few months earlier.

"Do you know what employee you replaced at the Coliseum? Graham!" She told me that our boss fired him because she was pretty sure he was the one who stole her television while she was at work.

Here's another odd part of the story: I later learned that Graham had been arrested for holding up a 7-11 store.

While in jail he became ill and an officer took him to the hospital. The officer obtained medical treatment for Graham and on their way back to the patrol car, Graham got away from him and made a b-line to my apartment complex.

The officer he escaped from was Ollie Carnes - the husband of a woman I'd worked with for a few years.

It was like everyone knew Graham but me...until now.

In hindsight I realize that my psychic skills were at work that day even though I didn't know it at the time. It was my guides who made me want to put my clothes nearby and it was my guides who assured me I would come out of this situation safely. I didn't learn about my guides or my psychic skills until years later.

And speaking of years later, another incident happened after I'd moved back to Odessa. I'd been living in Midland for 19 years after I was promoted to a supervisor position. I moved back to Odessa after my parents died in 1995. Actually I live in a rural area known as West Odessa. Odessa and Midland are only 20 miles apart.

West Odessa rarely has any criminal activity - most of the drama occurs in Odessa itself, so it was unsettling to me to learn that something bad happened only a few miles from my house.

A couple had a For Sale sign on their pickup truck. A man knocked on their door expressing interest in it. After they invited him inside to discuss it he pulled out a gun and tied them up so he could steal their valuables.

As he was gathering their possessions the lady's brother walked in suddenly and the man shot him. Fortunately her brother survived but was in the hospital for several months. The robber fled the scene in their pickup truck.

They found the abandoned truck on Interstate 20 halfway between Odessa and Midland. Apparently he'd escaped into the brush.

For some reason I couldn't quit thinking about it. I obsessed over it. They showed an artist's sketch of the man on TV - and it showed him wearing a baseball cap.

I thought to myself, "If I were that man I would lay low for the night, then hitchhike out of town the next day."

The next morning, I called in to work telling them I was going to take some leave but would be in that afternoon. Even though I lived in Odessa, my office was still in Midland. I was very sleepy that morning so I returned to bed.

When I awoke I "knew" I was going to help the police find that man. It was a very strong "knowing." My logical mind kept telling me that I was imagining things - why on earth would I have anything to do with the capture of this criminal?

In order to go to work I had to take the Interstate to get to Midland. As I neared the midway point between the two cities, I saw a man wearing a cap, hitchhiking west. I thought, "Nah....it can't be. Wayne, your imagination is warping your sense of logic."

But the feeling was overwhelming. After a few seconds I gave in and thought, "What the heck." So I used my cell phone to call the police. "I know I'm probably wrong but there's a man fitting the description of that man who shot that guy in West Odessa yesterday... hitchhiking in the west-bound lane of the Interstate halfway between Odessa and Midland."

After that I was able to put it out of my mind and didn't think about it again. I stayed late at work and got home just in time to see the 10 o'clock news. Not only was I right about the guy but my jaw dropped when I heard who it was: Graham Davisell!

I couldn't believe it.

I'd always wondered what happened to the young man who broke into my apartment when I was in my twenties.

He'd grown up and was still breaking the law.

I realize now that there must be some connection between him and me. I'd always resented the fact that he took something precious away from me by breaking into my apartment all those years ago: to this day I can't sleep the sleep of the innocent.... if I hear the slightest noise it wakes me up. I have to have every door and window locked and in place. He took away my sense of invulnerability and I resent it. For whatever reason I was allowed to give him some payback by arranging for his capture.

Sometimes I forget I'm psychic. My psychic skills aren't always obvious to me so when I'm channeling information like that I tend to discount it. My logical mind sometimes locks horns with my psychic mind. It was my guides who were at work pushing me to take notice of events that day.

Don't get me wrong. I don't hold grudges. I don't have seething resentment towards Graham Davisell other than the mild resentment that comes to me during lonely nights when I hear a sound that startles me awake. I haven't been dwelling on that day long ago when Graham invaded my life. I also have no idea why he and I crossed paths twice in a lifetime. He has no idea it was I who alerted the police because I didn't give them my name, but sometimes life gives us gifts and this was one of them.

Now, about my PAST LIVES:

When I was three years old, it came to me in a dream. I first saw myself by a stream, and I was wearing some sort of tunic but I didn't know that was what it was called. I just knew what it looked like. I knew I was in the beginning stages of love and it felt awesome; however to my three year old mind this was very confusing because who understands what that is at that age? I saw the sun glistening off the river and it was like diamonds.

I was an adult before I saw the rest of the memory. The next day in that life I followed my mother to the city square while she shopped for food. I was 16. I remember seeing the white government buildings with columns and steps. I also remember the vendors who sold vegetables and meats with the crowds and the noise. I was daydreaming and not really paying attention to anything.

BOOM! Something exploded behind me. I turned to gape at Vesuvius as it blew it's top. It came to me I was in Pompeii. The roar hurt my ears and I remember just standing there staring at it.

After a few moments I realized people were screaming and running in all directions. It occurred to me to run but I couldn't find my mother. It was at that point I realized my mother in that memory was my sister, Frances, today.

I started to run but didn't get far because I couldn't breathe. I was choking and then fell to the ground. As I left my body I was ANGRY. I was mad because I was young and we were wealthy and I had a great life. I was cheated. It was at that moment I realized this was where I got my 'all or nothing' attitude today.

Second memory:

That same night I saw another life. I saw myself standing in the kitchen and looking out to see a tornado not far away. The moment I saw it, it was all over. Seeing the storm launched my lifetime interest in tornadoes. To this day when I see one on television, I have to stop to take it in.

When I grew up I learned hypnosis because of my interest in reincarnation and my desire to explore these memories further.

One day a friend's daughter, Sam, had come to visit me because she was interested in hypnosis. I taught her what to do and asked her to regress me and she readily agreed.

When she induced a trance, she followed my instructions to help me explore any possible past lives. I immediately saw the tornado and got very emotional. The waves of feeling overwhelmed me which was a big surprise to me. She then instructed me to leave that situation, and to look for another past life…

Third past life:

The same night when I was three, I saw the third of my past lives. I saw red brocade wallpaper. I saw myself as a woman which surprised me. In that memory I was bitter about a man that I loved. I was sad and started crying and it woke me up. My older sister, Dixie, was staying with us while her husband, Jack, went on a ship somewhere (he was in the Navy). My crying woke her up and she asked, "Wayne, are you all right?"

I was already awake and still crying. When she spoke I froze and made myself stop crying. I pretended I was still asleep and didn't answer her. How could I? I had no idea how to explain what I'd just seen. I didn't understand why I saw myself as an adult woman, nor did I understand the feelings.

So when Sam instructed me to leave the memory of the tornado and go seek another memory, I went back to France where I saw the red brocade wallpaper again and realized I was in a bordello.

I was extremely angry and bitter. The anger washed over me and I'm afraid when Sam asked me her questions, I couldn't help but answer with venom. It was like being two people at the same time. I knew I was Wayne and knew I was intimidating Sam, but I was also that woman long ago who was angry at the world. In that life I had become mean and aggressive. It wasn't a good memory. When I revisited this memory later, I learned I had been guillotined.

One day I decided I wanted to know more about the tornado memory, so I decided to try self-hypnosis. I specifically wanted to know where I died.

I saw myself as a young person with reddish brown hair. I saw an old weather-worn, dusty sofa with a red textured fabric sitting on the porch that surrounded our house. The phrase "abject poverty" came to me. I was a little girl.

My next memory was that of a young girl. A neighbor boy named Jerry, who was plump and unappealing, had been badgering me about sex. At that point I gave in because I was curious. As we were comparing anatomies, my mother walked in and was furious. I was forced to marry this boy even though we didn't have sex. I'm afraid he got the bad end of the deal. I was unhappy and impatient with him, and I resented him intensely.

The next memory I saw was of me as an adult. Jerry had just gone somewhere in the car and our small son was with him. I was cleaning the kitchen. It was storming outside and when I sensed a change in the wind outside, I looked out the window in time to see a tornado about to hit.

It came to me that I died in "Wyandotte County near Kansas City." Having lived in West Texas all my life, the only thing I knew about the area was that there were two Kansas Cities. I grabbed the K encyclopedia (only because it was closer to me than the M (for Missouri). To my amazement I discovered that Kansas City, Kansas is the county seat of Wyandotte County.

For a few years I was passionate about reincarnation, so I often submitted to hypnosis or conducted self-hypnosis sessions. I learned I was a Catholic priest once and was a monk several times, both Catholic and Asian.

I saw myself as a Viking on one occasion and I had married a woman that I later learned was my mother in this life.

I learned that in some lives we are female and in some we are male. There is, in fact, no such thing as gender in Heaven although we can choose any appearance we want.

CHAPTER 26 GRAMPA'S GHOST

by I.G.

Grampa Joe passed in the early 80's and I was going out a lot then. About three days had gone by when he passed and I came home from going out that night. I fell asleep with my light on in the room and I was going into an alpha state of consciousness – very deep when I felt this nudge on my right shoulder and I turned to look to see who it was and I seen my grampa.

At that moment it dawned on me that my Grampa was dead. I thought wait a minute... grampa's gone! He can't be alive next to me!

Did my dead grampa speak to me?

No. But he wanted to! - but I had absolutely no awareness to spirits then.

The oddest thing I remember is when I was trying to go back to sleep I was not in a sleep, but tired. Sort of semi-conscious, and wow - there was my grampa's face appearing in my room! Very near me - and just by the look in his face he was trying to talk to me. Trying with that look on his face, I will never forget it ever… he was so desperately trying to tell me something! There was sort of a stern look in his face.

Unfortunately I had no knowledge or experience regarding this. I wasn't wise enough to say anything nice to him - I was in my selfish state in my 20's, so I looked at this odd ghostly distraction in my room and mumbled, "Leave me be," "I'm so tired I want to sleep."

Then at that very moment, it dawned on me this was not my imagination or some distraction but my real grandfather. I questioned the fact that, was he really here? as I was trying to go back to sleep. I said to myself, "Hey, wait a minute, is that really him?"

I sat up and looked over towards my closets and his face had moved back and now he was full body standing there in a glow-like light, almost sort of smoky looking. He almost looked as if you can see right through him.

Grampa was smiling then with a loving and peaceful face. I was surprised that he looked healthy and strong, and I got this vibe like he was proud of me for something I did. There was an eerie, loving, peaceful feeling in my room.

Realizing he was really with me, I got emotional looking at him. My eyes teared up. I didn't even say anything to him, but it was as if he was speaking to me with his whole being. No words exchanged - just mentally. I became comfortable not afraid of it, calm and a yet joyous.

Then I felt a presence of something other than him in the room, like an energy of something more powerful than what is on Earth, and the whole experience was probably time suspended. My life seemed small and like it didn't matter in comparison to this bigness. But I felt I mattered just that my little dramas and other people's dramas did not add up to anything crucial.

It really didn't last very long. If I knew now what I seen then things would have been different. I now question my love ones when I see them in my dreams for answers about spiritual things and I am very much loving when I see them in my dreams because sometimes they are not in my head but really there like grampa was.

CHAPTER 27   CHILDHOOD HABIT OF LEAVING MY BODY

by Scott B.

First I wanted to thank you so much for the book you wrote, *Forgiving Troy*. It was a tremendous, superb piece of literary work and I found it very inspiring to be open to forgiveness to everyone in our lives that have hurt us. I truly admire your courage in opening up your life to all to read and share, and you could feel the catharsis and growth you had on the path of writing this book.

Now on to the spiritual experience I had when I was younger. To set the background, when I was younger, I had the first of many out-of-body experiences. We were living in Wisconsin and there was a tornado warning in the middle of night and our family sought shelter in the basement. I was about seven years old, terrified and scared out of my wits when it happened.

I felt myself rising out of my body and I was watching the whole family like they were on television. I had a feeling of peace and serenity while all around was chaotic.

After this first time, I started practicing the ability on my own. At first I only seemed to be able to perform this psychic feat when I was in a stressful situation, but after some practice I was able to do it occasionally. Looking back on it as an adult, there was a time when I thought I was dreaming of certain travels but I think it was true astral projection! - as was the time when I traveled to each of the planets.

So now that I have set the background, my spiritual experience occurred in May, 1986. I was 17 years old and driving to a school function when a severe car accident occurred where I was rear-ended into traffic and hit from head-on, causing massive damage to the car. As a stupid teenager, I was not wearing a seatbelt so my chest was smashed into the steering wheel and column. In the process, I had a severe contusion to the heart causing my heart to stop.

As with previous stressful situations, I left my body and was in a position like being in a upper stadium seat watching the paramedics work on my injured body. Nothing felt any different at this time of my astral projection than previous experiences, until I had the strange feeling of another presence that I had never felt before when I projected my astral body.

This presence actually stood next to me and watched the scene below. I then turned to this presence and it was a female that looked familiar to me but I didn't know who it was. The presence then told me, "Scott, this is not where you belong at this time, you need to go back and resume living your life." With that being said I had this pulling feeling and I was back in my body and normal consciousness, being worked on my the paramedics.

After the situation, about six months later, at a family function there were old photos being shown and the female spirit I had encountered was there staring at me from a photo!

She was my paternal grandmother who had died when my father was 19 of cancer. I had never met her or seen her.

That was my little spiritual experience. I am glad I have been able to share it with someone.

CHAPTER 28   DOUSING

by J.M.

The only thing I can control is that I can douse for water, but it also picks up water lines, underground wires and large tree roots. I have doused and found water for wells. I have gone over a property dousing and marked the spot for the property owners. To see "If" I was right I asked them to tell me where the professional well diggers found water. They found water within a foot of where I told them to dig!

Dousing is easy; I'll tell you how to do it. Give it a try. 1st get two wire coat hangers, straighten them out, bend the hanger at 6 inches - you now have a long L. Take the hanger and measure out about a foot and cut it off. You now have an L shape 18 inches long. Make two of these. Hold them in your hands with just your four fingers, thumps pointed up. Hold your hands about 12 inches apart. Make the ends of the 12 inches point straight forward. Start walking through the area you're looking for water and the wires will cross when you walk over the spot that water is. To test this go to your water meter and trace the water line back to your house.

As for premonitions I can't control it. I have dreams about events; I don't know when they will happen, sometimes the next day, sometimes not for weeks. The one I have been having lately is about the banks going under, full depression. I had premonitions of airline businesses going under, months before they did.

CHAPTER 29   A CROSS APPEARS ON THE CEILING

by Harry M.

I actually had an out of body experience when I died for a minute on the operating table. Like many who had NDE's, it was wonderful, magical and otherworldly. A god presence was there to comfort me and answer questions - but I forgot the answers – had to. And I even saw my dead dog Scout who spoke a message to me. I recall his love but not the message – maybe the message was just love continues?

I also used to see ghosts when I was young, but it terrified me, so I asked God in prayer NOT to see anything again, and for the most part I have not. I have a friend from Dallas who was plagued by poltergeists in her home as a child (her mom can verify). They had to have a priest come and do an exorcism.

One night I ran away from my parents' house and slept at a friend's. Before I went to sleep (in the dark) I saw a big misty cross form on the ceiling of the room.

The next morning I looked at the ceiling and there was nothing there, so I could not understand why I imagined something so real. Suddenly at about 11 AM a friend came to the door, desperate, "You have to go home! Your parents are worried sick!"

I walked into an angry house because (long story) my girlfriend at the time had been killed at 2 AM the previous morning. I went to bed at 2 (no knowledge of her death) and that is when the cross had appeared to me. I am not a very religious person but do have a strong faith in God.

CHAPTER 30   BLOWN AWAY BY A PSYCHIC

by Angela Z.

Okay, Thom, where to begin?

I had a few connections with the other side through my friend Tricia Christo who is a Psychic Medium. I've been to Tricia's classes and watched her help so many people connect with their loved ones who have passed on or tell them what is going on or going to happen with loved ones who are here.

My first private reading with Tricia Christo was in Dec. 2005, a month after my father passed away. I was never close with him, he was absent most of my life.

Christmas Eve I was having a few moments to myself and I looked up and was wishing my mother a Merry Christmas, since she passed away when I was 7 months pregnant with my son, Nikolas. After I wished her a Merry Christmas I then said, "And you, too, Dad," meaning Merry Christmas to my dad, too.

Well like less than a week later I was at Tricia's house for my private reading and she was connecting with my parents. My father was coming through first and he told her to tell me thank you for what I said to him. Then when Tricia connected with my mother, her face started to look like my mother a bit around her eyes. Her face features changed! I've seen it more than once. It just amazes me how that happens. My mom wanted Tricia to let me know she sang with the king, that I needed to know that. When I say King I mean Elvis Presley. Cause if you remember years ago when Elvis died, rumor was going around he really did not die, he was alive, well my mom always said when I die I'll let you know if he is there. Well I guess she stuck to her word ;-) cause that was the very first thing she said.

My brother who turned 40 passed away in January, 2008. Tricia knew I was going through something and wanted to read me, cause she knew that gave me a lot of comfort. She told me my mother was standing next to me and rubbing my arm just as I felt my arm tingle and chill. The room got a bit misty.

That happens sometimes when a spirit enters a room. Also sometimes out of the blue I will smell the flower of gardenia, which I was smelling at that moment. There were no flowers in the room and the funny thing is that was my mom's favorite flower. She also told me my mom touches my head a lot. I do feel a light touch or like someone is rubbing my head out of the blue. When I was younger I use to lay my head on my mom's lap and she'd rub my head. It relaxed me and give me comfort.

I think everyone who has lost a loved one should see a psychic just once, they will see the comfort you get from the connection. When you have a private reading in person with Tricia you can bring photos of loved ones who have passed or are still here with us. One time I had a photo taken at the studio of my son when he was about two months old, as she was looking at it she pointed out an image in the photo - it was my mother's face.

There was my son's football photo with a ghost image in the background also.

My son sees his deceased grandmother all the time. He tells me how she comes in his bedroom and sits on his bed. One time my son was describing an additional elderly lady who was in his room, so I went and got a photo of my great aunt to show him. He said it was her. He never met her cause she died in 1996 and he was born in 1997.

CHAPTER 31   OF BROKEN WINGS

by Alex

Here is what happened following Scott's death (he passed on November 8 - two weeks after our anniversary)....

Since Scott's death I have had a real struggle with spirituality - his passing has really turned my belief system upside down. I have struggled with the notion that "this is it" – we have our brief chance at life here on Earth, and once we die, it is over. I think my studies in geosciences for two years at the University of Arizona have moved me pretty much to take the scientific view of life after looking at all those fossils in the layers of rock, but up until November, I had some spiritual base.

Scott's death had taken any shred of "spirituality" that I had managed to assemble, and threw it and me into some of the darkest places I have ever experienced, and I felt grief like I never even imagined possible.

After Scott died, I've been to Arizona several times, just to be near him – especially when I was having trouble with making important decisions. I feel a strange comfort being near his grave, even if it was just his body under the earth. He is buried at Paradise Memorial Gardens in Scottsdale.

Around Christmas, I had found some decorations to place on Scott's grave – a little Christmas tree, a Santa beanie character, and another one of a dog since he loved our dogs so much, and an angel made of ceramic. I also placed two mini solar lights at the head of his grave, with a couple of photos of Scott under Plexiglas just below the lights so that at night there would be a light that would shine on them. Paradise Memorial Gardens is a very unique cemetery in that sense – they encourage people to memorialize their loved ones in whatever way they choose. And so that is what I did. In some strange way, it enabled me to share Christmas with Scott.

I went to Arizona for 3-5 day segments each time, and so I would go from my mom and dad's place to the cemetery each day to have an hour or so of time to sit, meditate, and even "talk" to Scott (I'll admit, I only talked aloud when I knew I was alone). The most common thing I talked about was how painful it was for me to think that this was in fact the end – that I would never see him again, and would never have a chance to share our lives together again. I would openly say "I just want to know if you are okay " (I know, it does not make a lot of sense). But during all of this, we have a friend (Nancy) who claims she gets these "images" of people after they die – and she mentioned to me that "Scott was just fine" (I felt really uncomfortable and even a little manipulated with this, but there was some minor element of it that seemed to pull at me in a way that would allay my fears, however briefly).

On one of the windy days at the cemetery I was trying to keep the photos from blowing over. I tried to get the ceramic angel to "embed" in the ground next to them, and in doing so, I broke off one of the angel's wings, and slightly cut my hand. I was pretty upset and was frustrated with my emotions (and that day I had talked on the phone with our friend Nancy who said she had this vision of Scott and that "he's fine, and he's more worried about you, Alex"), and so I said aloud, "Scott, if you really are okay and there is something beyond what I can understand, then I want you to tell me."

I looked at the angel, and continued "I will come to terms with the notion that you are okay and that there is something beyond this life if someone brings up the concept of a broken angel wing on their own, and without any knowledge of this day." I am not sure why I threw out such a silly challenge, but I did it, and that was that.

I went home to my parents' place, and found some ceramic glue, and repaired the angel in my room and the next day took it back and placed in on his grave. I did not say a word about the angel to anyone, and my parents were unaware of the broken wing or anything to do with my discussion graveside that day (they would have thought I lost it if I told them anyway...)

This last week five friends took me to dinner at a place called Toast on 3rd for my birthday. I had mentioned that I did not want anyone to buy me gifts for my birthday – this was a year I just wanted to pass by, and I just wanted to enjoy their company as best as possible. But one friend did bring a gift (Tim), whose mother is now battling end-stage cancer. Anyway, Tim's gift was in a small rectangular box, and on the outside it read "Graphite Object," and on the end of the box it read "wing." It really did not even register with me as I opened the box. But when I lifted the lid and saw what was inside, I got this strange rush of emotion, and sat quietly for about 10 seconds until Tim (out of the nervous silence) said, "It's a piece of graphite – you can draw with it."

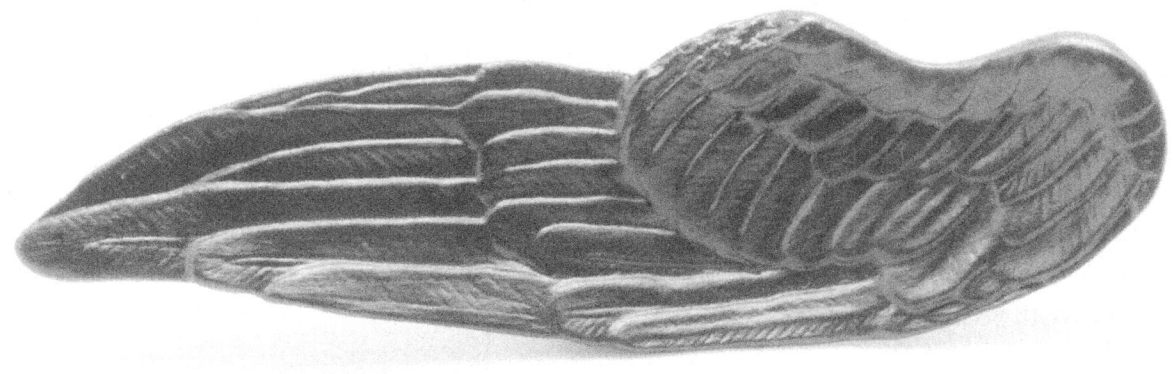

There is a very sweet write-up inside the box that reads:

"Wings have always inspired human awe, lifting and propelling birds, insects and mammals high above the cares and constraints on land. Mythology, poetry and religious texts commonly feature wings to attest to the bearer's speed or association with otherworldly realms. Wings hasten the feet of the Greek God Hermes, set a fairy about her magic, and allow angels to take humans under wing on earth and escort them to the heavens."

I still have a tendency to look at this as a big coincidence, but I admit it did make me feel better that day. If I stand back and look at it, there is a bit of a remarkable coincidence here – the first birthday without Scott, the first gift I had received for my birthday – in fact the first of anything since I made the request, and in a way, since I am an artist, the wing is of a material that would return me to my own work – drawing – sort of a message that it is okay to move forward….But again, there is that part of me that says it was just a very odd coincidence.

CHAPTER 32   MY DAD IS SET FREE

by Randy

The following story has special significance for me. I was living and working as a freelance illustrator in the third floor of a Victorian house on a quiet tree-lined street in Toronto in 1991. My dad died quite suddenly and I was given the unpleasant task of collecting his remains till we decided what to do. A day or so after returning home with my father's ashes, I distinctly heard the sound of footsteps in the hall while I was in the bathroom.

The first thought that came to mind was my dad. He had a habit of pacing up and down the hall when irritated. I remember thinking that even the pace of the footsteps sounded familiar. The footsteps continued several times daily throughout the week. I tried to rationalize what I was experiencing. I thought that because it had been such a stressful and emotional time that perhaps it could be my imagination.

The next odd occurrence happened towards the end of that week. It was a beautiful sunny afternoon with the light streaming through the windows giving a warm glow to the living room. I decided to take a break for a moment, give my eyes a rest from work and have a cup of tea. Suddenly, just as I placed the cup of hot steaming tea on the coffee table, my stereo and tape deck turned on by itself and began to play "Every Time We Say Goodbye" by Annie Lennox. Now it seemed strange that not only the stereo had turned on by itself but also that the tape deck also began to play. The remote was out of reach and the stereo 12 feet away from where I was sitting. I decided that someone or something wanted to hear the song so I let the song play through then got up and manually shut it off.

The following evening my mom phoned and I was telling her about the stereo and the song. As I was speaking to her I looked up and saw what I can only describe as a shadow of a bird moving across the ceiling towards the window. I heard the wings flapping and described what I was experiencing to my mom. Many years have passed since my father's death, and recently I asked my mom if she recalled that conversation. She clearly did. I still like to think that perhaps my dad was being set free or moving on to a better place.

CHAPTER 33   400 LB. MAN MAKES EERIE PRESENCE KNOWN

by Randy

About 15 years ago my brother Rick's daughter, Kathy, was dying of cancer, So to say the least my brother's mind was very occupied. This one morning Rick was leaving his home which was located in a smaller town outside of Toronto where he resided in a small suburb where people need cars to get around.

As he walked up to his car, he noticed this man sitting on the curb across the street. The man was an older gentleman who probably weighed 400 lbs. at the very least, Rick looked at the man and in return the man nodded back at him as to say good day.

My brother got in his car and looked around - there were no other cars nearby - how did this man get here and why is he just sitting on the curb? Rick then drove off and headed to the corner store where he needed a few things. As he drove away from the house he could see the man sitting on the curb in the rearview mirror.

When Rick reached the store and as he pulled up into the parking lot, the 400 lb. man was sitting in front of the store. Shaken by seeing the man there my brother kept asking himself how did he get to the store before him - but there he was sitting there – no cars around that he could have used to get there.

As Rick passed the man going into the store again, the man nodded at Rick, When he was leaving the store, the man was still outside the store sitting there.

Rick got into his car. As he started to back up he turned his head to look out the back window to finish his turn. When he turned his head around the man was gone. This shook him right up! Rick said there he was and then gone in an instant, a split second!

My brother sat there for a good 10 minutes before he started on his way home... As he drove down the road to the intersection where he would have to turn to go home there was a head-on collision where one of the drivers was killed. The accident happened 10 minutes before my brother approached the intersection.

Get this! - if my brother was not so shaken up by the bizarre circumstances he would not have taken the time to calm himself down and he probably would have been in that intersection when the crash happened!

So who was this 400 lb. man who just appeared twice out of nowhere and disappeared just as fast? - was it his guardian angel making him delay his drive back to his home – and save his life?

CHAPTER 34 THE GHOST WITH FALSE TEETH

by Cinda

Merom, Indiana. When my mom died in 1999, I bought out our family home from my brother and sisters with the intent to renovate and rent out.

A few years later, in May 2007, my youngest son and his family started renting from me. He knew the history already but he didn't care. My dad died from colon cancer in April 1997 in that house. He was diagnosed in June 1993 and after years of treatment, remission and in and out of the hospital for years, it had returned and the newest treatments were making him sick. He just wanted to go home to die. And he did.

My son's youngest daughter, Ally, was a year old when they moved in. In 2009, she was talking in her room one day. Her mom asked her who she was talking to. Ally said, "The pink man."

Her mom knew that when people had a tan or were dark-skinned, Ally referred to them as pink. Her mom questioned her further, playing along, and Ally said the pink man would smile at her and stick out his teeth.

Her mom told my son about it later and he was excited to talk to Ally about the pink man. After talking to her, he knew without doubt it was my deceased dad, his grandpa.

This was a game he played with all of the grandkids when they were very young. He had false teeth and would smile and stick them out. The grandchild he was playing with would try to grab them and he would close his mouth. The grandchild would laugh and laugh. So my son showed her a picture of my dad and asked her if she knew who that was. She said yes, it was the pink man. My son was very happy that my dad was around and Ally knew him even though he had never seen him or experienced any encounters.

CHAPTER 35   MOMMY, THAT WAS THE MAN IN MY ROOM

by Randy S.

Many years ago my sister was married to her first husband and gave birth to two daughters, Liz and Marley. Shortly after the birth of her younger daughter Marley, sis separated from her husband and started to raise her two year-old and one year-old on her own. Her ex-husband never came around again. The day he left was the last time he saw his daughters.

About a year later my sister met a new man and as time passed they moved in together and she gave birth to a son. They raised all three children as her new husband's children, never telling the daughters they had a different father. Being as young as they were when there real father left they had no memory of their natural dad.

Many years later when Liz was about eight years old, in the middle of the night she ran into her parents room screaming and crying out, "Mommy!! There's a man in my room!!"

Both my sister and her husband got up checked the entire house – but every window and every door was locked. There was no way any man came in and locked up when he left. They finally settled Liz down, convinced she had had a bad dream.

Later that morning my sister's phone rang. It was her former mother-in-law calling to tell her that her ex-husband had died earlier that morning in his sleep.

My sister had to break the news to her daughters that the father that they knew and loved was really not their father and that their biological father had passed away and they needed to say good-bye to him at the funeral.

The day of the service, my sister took her two daughters up to the casket at which time Liz replied, "Mommy, that's the man that was in my room." Liz had tried to describe the man that night when he appeared in her room but all she could say was he had curly hair and wore red and black checkers.

After the service my sister was shaken by her daughter recognizing her ex as the man in her room so she decided to call her ex mother-in-law and asked her what time did her ex actually die. She answered about 3 AM. It was about 3:30 AM when Liz had awoken them.

My sister then asked what he was wearing when he passed and was told a red and black checkered shirt.

Liz is now an adult and has pictures of her biological father and to this day says that that was the man in her room that night.

CHAPTER 36   POP POP APPEARS OUT OF NOWHERE

by Cinda

I was born in Baltimore Maryland in 1970. My paternal grandparents were nicknamed Nanny and Pop Pop. My grandfather being a Navy Veteran, I don't have very many memories of him, because my mother had left my father when I was 2. Now being almost 50, I have heard many stories of how Pop Pop was.

My mother told me the events of how my grandfather got shot. He was driving a hearse in Baltimore city and some people accused him of cutting them off. They forced him to the ground and shot him in the neck. This paralyzed him and confined him to a wheelchair in his late 20s, early 30s.

Mom added that her father, who suffered greatly from PTSD being a Viet Nam Veteran, wasn't a calming voice of reason - so my mother planned on moving back to Wisconsin where her family was from. That was around '72-'73. There were tensions being on both sides of my family.

A kid in Wisconsin, I went 12 years or so living a normal country life in Wittenberg, a town of less than 1,000 people.

The year was 1984. I was 14 and we had moved to a town of 300 named Sullivan, Indiana. My room was a normal teenager's room. Band pictures all over my walls. Only one wall was bare. My room was my sanctuary. My own private space. I went 12 years or so not able to talk to my grandfather because my parents relationship and divorce was bitter.

I was sitting on my bed probably listening to music and or doing homework. That part I don't remember but something made me pay attention to my only bare wall. Suddenly an apparition came onto the wall - it started off blurry. I guess the best way to describe is when you are watching a soap opera and a character remembers things and the pic gets blurry to give the viewer distinction of past events. It wasn't like a hole on my wall opening up. It was more of several pieces of a picture all coming together. The image was not tangible. No energy balls. No rigid jagged edges – but like soft, fluid pieces of a puzzle all coming together. Just like watching a movie on a screen. The vision didn't say anything but Pop Pop had the biggest smile on his face.

It was my grandfather in his wheelchair and he was smiling. The picture didn't say anything and only lasted a couple seconds. It didn't bother me. I was puzzled if you can excuse the pun. I didn't tell anyone either. People have a tendency of thinking one is crazy for these things. So about a week later I was horse-sitting for some friends. It was a weekend of solitude for me. The phone rang. I answered it. It was my mother on the other end telling me that my father had just called and explained my grandfather had passed.

He was only like 60 from what I've been told. So with the vision a week earlier now I was really starting to analyze. I truly believe that it was my Pop Pop coming through to say good-bye to his granddaughter that he hadn't seen in 12 years.

I cherish that vision - whatever it was. Being that was my first encounter of something out of the norm, I took it as special from the get go. Through the years I have gotten feelings that weren't quite normal but nothing has compared to my Pop Pop saying goodbye in his own special way.

His passing in 1984 which I could not attend, only heightened my wish to go to Maryland. Which I did in 1992 after serving 4 years in the Air Force. My Pop Pop is buried in a Veteran cemetery. He received a salute.

CHAPTER 37 GRANDFATHER'S CHAIR

by Bobby F.

After an extended illness with Multiple Myeloma, my grandfather passed away on Jan. 23, 2001. I was living where I still do in Austin, Texas, and my family was all back in East Tennessee (well, that's where my mother's family was, I have no idea where my father's family was -- and still don't -- since he is no longer part of my family).

My mom called me early in the morning of Jan. 23rd and said that she and the rest of the family had been called to the hospital so I suspected the worst. After praying for a while, I dozed off back to sleep and I had a dream that my grandfather was sitting in his favorite recliner back home.

That is the only thing I remember from the dream.

Just him sitting peacefully in his recliner.

A few minutes later (it seemed like I had been asleep much longer), my mom called me back and said that he had passed away.

Later that night, I called and told her about my dream.

She shared with me that before she left his hospital room the final night before he passed away, he grabbed her arm and said, "Be careful."

He had never said that to her before any of the other times she left, so we think he knew he was leaving.

My mom has had many dreams of my grandmother who passed away in 1984 and said that her mom was often reassuring her about life circumstances and offering advice.

CHAPTER 38 TOUCHED BY AN ANGEL

by Kathy P.

In 2008 I lost my father to Alzheimer's Disease, and while he was in the nursing home, Mom was diagnosed with kidney disease that led to her having dialysis every other day. I promised my dad that I would take care of Mom the day he died. So three of my four brothers and I made sure she was taken care of - which meant every other day a trip for four hours to have her blood cleaned. It began to wear her down which was really hard to watch as my mother was very active both physically and in our small community of Ludlow Falls, Ohio.

Mom and Dad had lived in this town for over 50 years of their 60 year marriage. In 2012, on our way to dialysis, she just came out and said she was ready to be with Dad. I kind of just laughed and said it wasn't her time and she had more time to be with us. Then I looked into her tired hazel eyes and said, "Mom, when you do go, will you please come back and let me know that you are ok?"

She kind of just laughed it off and quickly changed the subject. In June, when one should be thinking of summer days and nights, I was thinking of how to make my mother more comfortable. She was admitted to the hospital for a few days for nutrition and her kidneys. In that time, she had a slight heart attack and the hospital didn't catch it. I know this because a week after being released, she was right back in there again. She couldn't keep anything in her system.

At a different hospital the doctors told us that she has a blockage and they were going to open her up and find it. After surgery, they told us kids that when they opened mom up, she was all hardened inside. Like she was totally crystallized inside and she wasn't going to make in through the night.

Well, she made it through the night and most of the morning - and then we let her pass away. The next morning, with the birds singing and sun shining, I didn't want to go alone and make her funeral arrangements. My brother came over for coffee and to go with me. I wasn't dressed when he got here, I was still in my old green bathrobe. My kitchen was quiet. All you could hear was the clock ticking as we just sat there in silence. I had just put out a cigarette and all of a sudden I felt two hands grab my arms through my robe and a really warm feeling on my neck as if it were a warm hug.

I just knew it was my mom telling me she was okay. A calmness came over me and I felt comfort from whatever just touched me. It was mom... I just knew it.

I didn't tell my brother about it until a month after her death, and he said he had not felt anything when I did.

I feel blessed for that one special moment. And I have never ever felt anything like it since. I was indeed touched by an angel.

CHAPTER 39   NAGGED WITH FEELING SOMEONE NEEDS RESCUE

by Nancy

We lived in Paulding, Ohio and it was in the Spring. I was a Licensed Practical Nurse working in Defiance, Ohio and worked 1st shift. It was about 20 years ago. I was a single mother of three sons. One afternoon after work I came home as usual and the boys were outside with their friends. I was standing in my kitchen washing dishes that were left behind and looking out the kitchen window. Suddenly I felt weak and this feeling from literally the top of my head to my toes gave me a feeling of dread, and a "silent voice" in my thoughts told me "someone you love needs you."

I stopped washing the dishes, ran outside to find my sons and checked on neighbors with this feeling, but everyone was all right. I "tried" to continue my day with this nagging feeling in my heart and thoughts, but I couldn't shake it. Meantime, my friend invited us over to her house that evening in Defiance and I accepted.

Couple hours later, early evening, the kids and I were driving my Dodge Stratus to Defiance, and I still had this gut feeling someone needed my help. As we were driving down by the river I suddenly took a left turn into my Mother's neighborhood, out of the blue. So we pulled up to her house and the kids ran in before I did.

In a few seconds one son yelled, "MOM!!! Granny is on the floor really sick vomiting and needs YOU!"

Thom, I ran in there like a bullet to find my now 88 year old mother crawling on the floor saying, "I have been trying to call you but I have been too sick to get to the phone. I need to go to the hospital - please don't leave me!"

THAT was WHO needed me! I completely felt "that intuition, phenomenon, whatever we call it." It had gone straight through my body telling me someone needed MY help! Something made me turn my car to the left suddenly after hours of that feeling. Needless to say we got my mother to Promedica Defiance Regional Hospital around 7.30 PM with a migraine and everything turned out well. Hard to explain, but so true...

Thom, that experience was the strangest creepy feeling that literally crept thru my body from the top of my head to my feet, I can't even explain that sensation of doom.

EMPATH

NO EMPATHY

CHAPTER 40   UNEXPLAINABLE SCREAMING

by Randy

So many years ago, back in 1987, my grandmother whom I called Nanny lived with her sister Florence, who passed away that year. Flo's kids wanted to sell the house so we had to move Nanny out right away. She went to stay at her granddaughter Darlene's home.

Nanny and her sister, Florence, were Jehovah's witnesses and had very strong faith in their religion. After the funeral my Nanny and her other sister, Betty, were upstairs in bed while about 10 of us were in the living room discussing the funeral services. My sisters and I were saying we liked the service, how they were saying Florence is sleeping and one day Jesus will call for her resurrection. My brother-in-laws were arguing, saying, "Are you crazy? The Jehova's don't take blood if they need it… they don't do this they don't do that,,, " It was getting to become a heated argument. Thru the high voices my sister, Darlene, stood up and shouted, "Stop it, guys!"

As she said this, a woman's scream went throughout the house. It wasn't like it was coming from anywhere in particular. It was like it was right there inside the room. From someone invisible?

To check, me and my sister Dar went up to my Nanny's room where she was sound asleep, Betty was reading a book in bed next to her. We asked did my Nanny cry out in her sleep?

"No," she replied.

None of us could figure out where the scream came from, but from that day on my sister's house was haunted to the point no one would sleep over there, including me.

Later we were telling my mom what happened that night of the funeral and Mom chuckled and kiddingly said, Well, if that really was a spirit screaming in your house, when I die I'll scream through your house, too."

Two years later my mother passed away from a massive heart attack. The night of her funeral we were at my other sister Liz's for the wake.

Back at my sister Darlene's house, Christine, her daughter, and her friend were babysitting a little brother. Reno, who is Darlene's husband, decided to leave the wake early and go home and check on Christine and their son. When he got home he found Christine and her friend hysterical and crying on the front steps of the house. Reno asked what was wrong. Christine told him they were playing cards when out of nowhere a woman's scream went thru the house.

My mother was a person who was terrified of death, I mean terrified. I think her fear was built on, "What if there is nothing after death?? - that this is it - and it all ends??" So in a very positive way it gave us some peace of mind knowing after the screaming she knew there was more and for sure was not afraid anymore. If it was her screaming in the afterlife, she only screamed once, probably to keep her promise. We kind of figured she was letting us know, like she said she would.

CHAPTER 41   A MAGIC GOURD FROM DAD?

by David

I was a pale, blond, blue-eyed round-cheeked little ham of a kid who wanted a lot of attention, the "star" of every situation -- (ohh, would that change in later years!); in pictures I'm always smiling or laughing or just hamming it up. We lived in a small 3-bedroom one-story rambler in a southern Indiana suburb called New Albany; I shared a room with my brother, but I don't remember exactly what it looked like -- just two twin beds, a couple of other pieces of furniture, etc.. When I was a little kid, like 6 and 7 years old, I used to have floating-visions when I'd lie down to go to sleep. I wasn't yet asleep, but when I'd close my eyes, I'd see visions of weird, random Peter-Max-meets-Salvador-Dali type images. It's been a while, so the pictures are hard to describe in detail, particularly without me sounding nuts.

Even then (as now), I had a hard time falling asleep, but these images would keep me entertained so that I would stay in bed. It was like watching an odd-yet-entertaining slide show projected onto my eyelids.

I've never told anyone about it, because I don't know what it was. And because I was on tranquilizers in first grade (Thom, I think I told you that?), I've wondered if it was a drug-induced vision -- Valley of the Dalis?

I cried every day when I had to leave home! I had severe separation anxiety and for some reason was afraid that if I left the house, that comfort and security would go away while I was gone. And I had an over-developed sense of empathy, I think (still do, in a way) -- if other kids got in trouble in school, I'd be the one to get distraught and start crying, because I felt the upset that I thought they would feel inside, if that makes sense. I just wanted everything and everyone to be calm, stable, and happy.

Interestingly, the visions abruptly stopped when I started being sexually abused at age 7. (OK, talk about bringing down the mood...) The visions may have stopped because I became more focused on tensions and fears. And I never ever got the visions back. The abuse... oy, family member... not much more I want to say about it. I've been through therapy, hypnosis, dealt with it to the best of my ability, but irony of ironies, I'm still protecting the abuser's anonymity and peace of mind.

My dad died in 2002, (who was not the abuser but I bring him up now because I want to share another unexplainable event) out of the blue. He got sick with a rare type of cancer called multiple myeloma (Peter Boyle had it; Roy Scheider died of the same thing); Dad was diagnosed at 62 and died at 65. He was truly the healthiest guy I knew, doing everything "right" to safeguard his mental and physical health, so the diagnosis was absolutely shocking and turned my world upside down. Until a couple weeks before he died in August 2002, I never gave up hope that he would beat that damn disease. He died in Minneapolis, at home. I was still lost and sad and very much missing him. He had a very calming presence. He could talk me down from the ledge, so to speak, and we had a very similar, skewed sense of humor. Dad loved words, wordplay, puns, and he was the type of guy who would, on a whim, take the afternoon off work, come by the house and get me, take me horseback riding (of all things!), then go back to work. He was a cool combination of quixotic and pragmatic.

Two months after he died, on a clear cool October night, I went to Vons in Studio City with a friend, and in the produce section saw this big basket of gourds. Before he died, my dad had taken up gourd-painting as a hobby. He was very much into southern folk art type handicrafts. He found designs in art books, or made them up in his head -- usually just patterns, colors, almost tribal-looking; he'd make them for my nieces and nephew too, but they'd have funny ghost-faces painted on them for Halloween, or he'd paint fish -- he loved to fish and was actually a really talented artist. A frustrated artist, who probably didn't belong in the corporate world but wound up there to support his family. He never sold the gourds, just gave 'em as gifts to friends and family. In fact, I have this little felt-lined hollowed-out gourd he made. The gourd itself is a dark tan color, and the paint is red, royal blue, light blue, white, and there's a row of fish around the bottom; he lined it with butterscotch-colored felt; attached a bead and string at the top, so the "lid" is easy to remove, and I keep rings in it. I treasure it on my nightstand.

In Vons, I was going to buy a gourd as a tribute to Dad, but I stopped myself. "It'll just remind me of him and make me too sad," I told my friend. So I went through the checkout, put my groceries in the trunk. When we returned to the apartment, I popped the trunk, and there, resting not in but on top of the very front bag, was this one perfect gourd. I hadn't bought it. My friend assured me she hadn't bought it -- I know, most people will think she did. All I can tell you is that she's our upstairs neighbor, I'd known her for over 2 years at that point, an Iowa transplant -- good Midwestern stock -- and she's very honest. She lost her younger brother unexpectedly a few years prior to my dad's death, so she "gets it," and she's not one to mess around with people's feelings when it comes to this kind of stuff. Plus, the truth is that I went through the checkout line ahead of her, I was in command of my cart and groceries the whole time, I loaded them, my bags were in the trunk and she put hers in the backseat; I was never not "in charge of" my bags, and my friend simply didn't have the opportunity to sneak the gourd. Additionally, although I mentioned the gourd to her, I don't think I conveyed the real significance to her. And in fact she was as shocked as I was. She gasped, looked startled, wide-eyed, and uttered her response to all thing surprising -- "Are you kidding me?!"

I'm not horrible at reading people, and I think I'd know if she were feigning surprise. It gave me goose bumps! Was it my dad's way of communicating with me and telling me to not be sad? I don't know. I guess I can come up with ways to dismiss this -- e.g., a previous customer had bought the gourd, left it behind, and the bagger had accidentally put it in with my items parcel instead. But then why wouldn't I have seen it when I loaded my groceries -- especially if it was right on top of, and not down inside of, that bag? It was a very pale tan gourd. Just like the ones he used to paint. I don't have any answers -- just the anecdote.

This is all very interesting, as it comes at a time when I've discovered (to my extreme chagrin) some unpleasant things about my dad (courtesy of my mother, who feels compelled to share some shocking and intimate things about him, despite all three of us kids pleading with her to write it down, tell it to a priest, tell anyone but her children!), things that have caused me to step back from missing him and to feel a lot more cynical about him. Very soap opera-ish things have come to light, truly. But in a way, just recounting this has made me smile and remember the good feelings instead of focusing on the fresh wounds.

CHAPTER 42   INVISIBLE HAND SAVES MY LIFE

by Zach Milan

In 2003 I was working on the Sony Studios lot which used to be the old MGM studios. It was a god-themed picture titled *Joan Of Arcadia*. The first assistant director Laura and I used to constantly try to drink 8 bottles of water a day. Of course in doing so this led to several trips to the restroom. So I ran out of the soundstage - was trying to run to the restroom and return to the stage as fast as I could. The restroom on the lot had narrow steps leading up to it which were concealed by a wooden partition.

I finished in the restroom, washed my hands and I ran down the stairs with no view of the alley. As I got to the bottom step, somebody grabbed me by the by arm and pulled me back just as a heavy, loaded golf cart driven by two large men went speeding by, inches ahead of me.

I would have definitely been run over. My first thought was that maybe there was a grip or electrician or someone else on our crew that I knew that was in one of the stalls who grabbed me but of course that was impossible. There were no open areas or doors where I stood – this was a typical solid staircase from an alley to an upstairs bathroom. Nevertheless I searched the restroom and found I was absolutely all alone, nobody else was in there. In a situation such as this I just kept trying to think of a logical explanation. Somebody forcefully grabbed me – who? How? But there was only one narrow set of stairs leading up to the restroom - there was no other way a human could have gotten to me.

Slowly I walked back to the soundstage and I was pretty freaked out. I had to tell somebody so I talked to our second A.D. Velvet who was a close friend. She said let me see your arm. I took off my long sleeved shirt, I had on a t-shirt underneath, and there were bruises on my bicep. it looked like a thumbprint and fingers. That made it clear that something forcefully grabbed me.

I thought that I either had a guardian angel or some crew member from another era (1940s or 1950s?) was killed in the exact same way by being struck by a vehicle - and saved my life

CHAPTER 43   DOES NOT LIKE TALKING ABOUT THE GHOST

by Joe

Years ago, a friend and I had gone to a party on the west side of Los Angeles. I dropped him off at his house kind of late. I had an aversion to driving all the way to my house, which would have been a long drive, especially after having had a few drinks at this party. My friend was nice enough to offer me his couch to sleep on, so I wouldn't have to make the drive.

He provided me with a pillow and blanket and I proceeded to make myself comfortable on his couch. I left the living room light on so that if I had to get up in the middle of the night I wouldn't be tripping over anything. I remember closing my eyes, just on the verge of sleep, when I had the feeling that someone was looking at me. My eyes were shut - but have you ever had the sense that someone was looking at or staring at you? I thought perhaps it was my friend goofing around or playing a joke. I opened my eyes and to my surprise, the room was empty. Right after I opened my eyes, however, I could hear footsteps walking away from me and out of the room.

I watched the sounds of the floor creaking. No one was there! I could hear definite distinct footsteps walking away. I couldn't see anything, but definitely heard it. The hair on the back of my neck stood up, as I clearly knew what that was – a ghost. It was difficult but I eventually fell asleep.

The next morning, I told my friend what I had experienced and explained to him that I didn't think it was my imagination. I knew that what I had heard had to have been a ghost or spirit. He told me that it wasn't my imagination, that he had similar experiences in the house which he didn't like to talk about. It was an old house, built around 1910.

I had an intense curiosity all my life to know if ghosts were real – and this answered my question.

CHAPTER 44   HOPING FOR MOM BUT GRANDMA COMES

by Pattie

My mother passed in 2009. Two years went by and there was nothing I felt was communication with her. Then one night I was watching Chris Daughtry guest starring on *Americam Idol* and the second he started singing, one of my cats started meowing like crazy - from being in a sound sleep. I picked him up and sat back down trying to keep him quiet - but he kept looking over my shoulder meowing. I turned to look twice and there was nothing at all there. I had a strange feeling, like someone was watching me. Then he calmed down and went to sleep like nothing happened.

Sharing this the next day with my boss, he assessed it was my deceased mom visiting – but how could we be sure? Nothing happened afterwards to confirm this.

A couple years later when I visited the cemetery and asked my mom's tombstone if I really was visited that night - to prove it to me and do it again. So that evening I was in the kitchen making dinner and ran to the TV announcing Daughtry guesting again on *Idol* – a remarkable coincidence, right? Synchronicity. He started to sing and that moment my cell started ringing. Normally I would've ignored it but answered even though I didn't recognize the number. It turned out to be my boss's mother. It was a different boss than before as I had changed jobs. Old boss gave her my number as a few months before I had pet-sat for him. So she said she had no clue why she called me, she hit the wrong number, made small talk and hung up just as Daughtry was finishing. Just like my cat stopping at the same time two years before. It didn't even dawn on me until hours later that the timing was perfect and it was a mother. Not mine - but a mother nonetheless. A mother appearance you might say. So although none of this was concrete evidence my Mom was in spirit next to me, these bizarre coincidences convinced me an effort was made to respond to my plea at her tombstone earlier that day.

Fast forward to the Christmas before Daughtry had a part in that Fox live broadcast at Easter. I was on the couch reading about it and read it out loud to the cats (as if they cared) and as I did out of the corner of my eye I saw the flicking candles that you twist on start to light up. Now they are on the mantle year round and that has never happened before or since.

Anyway the next time was when I was on the way to Cleveland for a meet & greet before the show. There was noooooo reason for this as again it has never happened before or since but my Daughtry CD kept repeating the same tracks. Freaked me out.

The following year there was a New Age Fair downtown Buffalo so I planned ahead and researched the psychics. I chose a medium and paid for a 15 minute reading. She was amazing. She knew that I lived in the mountains in the past (Utah) and other things very few people know. So I asked about the visitations and that I thought it was my mom. She was CERTAIN that it was not – that instead it was my maternal grandmother. Hard for me to believe since I never met her - she passed when my mom was 21 which was 10 years before I born. I didn't believe her.

When I was leaving, the psychic grabbed hold of my hand and said she was being told to ask me if during these episodes if I had smelled the scent of roses. I did not recall that, but figured she tapped into my mom who had a rose garden in the backyard at one time. But the psychic still believed it was related to my grandmother. That was in February.

In April I was driving to NYC and thinking about the reading when it hit me like a brick. The medium asked me about roses - my grandmother's name was ROSALIE!!!!

CHAPTER 45   GHOST VOICE TELLS ME TO LOCK MY CAR

by Anonymous

March, 1995. On my birthday I thought I was supposed to meet my sisters for a celebration dinner at La Rustica in New Westminster, BC, Canada. The restaurant was on a busy road with little parking available, so I drove down a side street and parked.

When I got to the restaurant I realized I was at the wrong place so I had to go back for the car and head to the right restaurant. What I didn't realize was that a tall, overweight man carrying a cup quietly began to chase me once I was back on the dark side street. In a dress and high heels, I arrived at my Toyota Tercel totally unaware that I was in trouble. I got in and immediately I heard a voice in my head say "lock your door" and I instantly did. I never locked my door!

No sooner had I locked my door this big man was at my window and he was winded like he had been running after me. He was seething and he yelled at me "GIVE ME SOME MONEY!!!" and he hovered over me, crazed. I was stunned and leaned back yelling that I didn't have any money. He looked down at my car door lock to see if I had locked it and he saw that I had.

In that moment I started the car and drove off. God knows what that man would have done to me if I hadn't locked that door in the split seconds I had to do so. That voice in my head saved me. Not sure if were my deceased parents guiding me or a Guardian Angel? There were lots of trees and bushes around so I would have been in big trouble. I was lucky to have reached my car in time and lock it. Like I mentioned I never locked my car but a voice instructed me to. That aggressive man meant business and he was angry! A clear voice saved me. A spirit guide intervened.

CHAPTER 46   MUSEUM SCHOLAR SEES A NOVA SCOTIA PIRATE SHIP

by George B.

I was born in Toronto, the second of four children and spent all my summers at the family cottage in Nova Scotia where my parents were originally from. When I was 10 we moved back to the east coast and I stayed there until I was 23. Then I moved to Ottawa, Canada's capital, to attend college and begin my career. I've since worked in the museum field for 24 years. I presently live in an old stone house in the village of Merrickville, Ontario, with my partner of 12 years.

Growing up in the Canadian Maritimes, a belief in things other than the three-dimensional world we occupy was as valid a belief as any scientific explanation. The eastern provinces have always been known as the most haunted part of Canada due to their longer history of settlement. Many friends and acquaintances I went to school with accepted as quite normal (but odd) stories of someone's house containing a poltergeist, or having seen a ghost, or having a relative who could see "signs" or portents of upcoming events.

My own experiences were varied and the psychic stuff far more common when I was younger. I do believe that as we mature we tend to become skeptical and put aside the beliefs we had as children, and doubt or even deny experiences that we cannot easily explain.

Luckily I have always been skeptical of everything I'm presented, right from my earliest memories, and I believe that skepticism has served me well in life.

My maternal side of the family was descended from the many poor Irish and Scots who were forced from their lands by the British and came to North America for a chance at a better life. They brought many of their old ways with them. Although they were Christians, these immigrants still carried a strong belief and cultural memory of their Pagan roots.

One of these beliefs was that certain people are gifted as the receivers of visions as well as the ability to interpret them. My mother would tell me stories of her grandmother who was the seventh daughter of a seventh daughter. In the old Celtic religions, this made her "fey" or a seer. That word once held special status and respect and it was only the Christian missionaries and the British who changed the word to something derogatory.

I truly believe, as my mother did, that some of that "gift" was passed on to her, and to some extent myself. My mother's clearest story of this ability was when she decided to elope and take the train from Nova Scotia to Toronto where my father had moved to find work. On the train she fell asleep and she said she had the oddest dream where she saw a one-armed man bowling. She laughed it off until she arrived at the boarding house where my father was living and met the couple who had taken him in. My father had mentioned nothing to my mother about his hosts, and here was the husband, who had lost an arm, telling my mother how much he enjoyed bowling.

For my part, I've always had the dilemma of trying to decide the difference between worry, healthy paranoia, and actual visions. This requires a bit of explanation: everyone "thinks" we know this, but we rarely ask each other how it actually occurs or feels like. Personally, my mind is like a television. It seems to be constantly on – even while I sleep. To say it's busy would be an understatement! There's the physical world to maneuver through, problems to be solved, dangers to be avoided, situations to be assessed in seconds, and reactions to be gauged constantly – all this on our own plane of existence. While all this is going on, my mind chugs along in the background, sending me images, thoughts, sounds, music, moods. The best way I can describe it as a fleeting sight of a screen, like watching a movie. My "job" is to interpret all these stimuli and to be honest. During the day that's rather difficult as the tangible world really does require a lot of our attention.

Being able to be mindful of the other senses going on in my mind is, like it is for many people, easier to do at rest, in isolation, or when we're sleeping. We already know the mind goes through several stages during our rest and sleep so it makes perfect sense that our brains take advantage of those times to get our attention. I've never been able to "clear my thoughts" as I have read many times. There's just too many going on at the same time, and do I really need to do that to relax? When I fall asleep, the non-stop messages in my mind just seem to go down in volume a few notches. Of course, once I'm unconscious, the real fun begins in dreams.

I see a real difference between being able to see, if only fleeting, a glimpse of the other planes of existence or time, and the brain's replaying of the days events and our concerns, through symbols. Other people have put a great deal of effort into studying these symbols and I'm not going to get into that here. My point is that the ability to "see" the other and the future (or past) is not the same as the mind's replaying the day's events or our concerns. The big task, the way I see it, is to be able to differentiate between the two.

For instance, I commute an hour to work each way, every weekday. I like to drive fast (but carefully) and I am always wary to look for police cruisers, to avoid getting speeding tickets. Experience with tangible events tells me where they might be parked, and when, but every so often I will get a "notice" from my mind telling me that there is a police car a few miles up the road coming in my direction. Sometimes this turns out to be the case, and sometimes not. I have to learn the difference, as I've said earlier, between a real premonition, and simply worrying that I will be stopped for speeding.

This isn't a very impressive example, but I wanted to describe how I believe my mind, and possibly those of others, works. As a skeptic would say, "If you can predict the future, why don't you tell me the winning lottery numbers for this week?" I don't think premonitions work that way at all. We have to truly desire some knowledge of upcoming events or an event that has happened that we don't know about yet. Winning the lottery isn't really that important to me, and I don't give it any thought, so it's not a wish of mine to know how it will turn out.

Sometimes this gift works in other rather uninteresting ways that I think many people are capable of: we've all heard stories about people who were thinking of someone and suddenly they phone. I have the odd ability to know, maybe eight times out of ten, who is calling when the phone rings, or as soon as I touch the phone itself.

As far as paranormal experiences go, most can be explained away by the empiricists out there, but not all, and I remain convinced that there is more to our reality than we fully understand: a concept that all scientists should appreciate since any fact starts from a theory.

Here are several:

Like most children in the 1960's in North America, I fell victim to all the usual childhood maladies…mumps, measles, whooping cough, etc.. I remember clearly when I had the measles and was home from school, my mother bundled me up and put me in my parents bed so she could watch me while she did her ironing in the same room. I remember falling in and out of a feverish sleep; somewhere between consciousness and sleep. My mother had left the room and in the sunny brightness of mid-afternoon, I distinctly remember waking up to see the skeleton of a small child leaning on the foot of the bed. It didn't move, but it spoke to me through my mind. It was quite friendly and it was asking me to go and play with him. Something instinctively told me this would be a bad thing to do, and I realized that this was Death. In that instant, it vanished. Of course, you could easily pass this off as a hallucination caused by a fever, but I think otherwise.

While I have never actually seen a ghost with my own eyes, I have certainly felt and heard them. I grew up in what had been an 1840's farmhouse. During the Second World War, many German POW's were sent to Canada and if you had a farm that needed laborers, you could put them up in exchange for the help. Most were treated very kindly, even in the camps, and many returned to Canada when the war was over. My family had two such men staying at the house, in the back, which later became my bedroom. When we moved into the house my father started to renovate it. Once thing he did was to block up the tiny circular back stairs that went from the kitchen to the room I shared with my brother. For some reason, I thought it was a really bad idea to enclose a staircase that now went nowhere. I couldn't explain why I thought this was wrong, it just "felt" wrong.

Soon after this, I was in bed one night sleeping, my bed was now at what had been the top step. I awoke and distinctly heard footsteps coming up the stairs. Terrified, I pulled the covers over my head and winced to make the sound go away, which it eventually did. On another night, I heard breathing in the room, and when I realized that the rest of my family were all away, again, I pulled up the quilts and hoped it would go away. I later learned that one of the POW's had internal injuries that no one had spotted and he died in that room.

During my teens I met and made friends with three people who are close to me still. Two of them are quite open to the supernatural, but the third is convinced that nothing is stranger than reality – we don't need to make up ghosts and such. We were all out at a cottage on a lake that one of them had in their family. It was a bright sunny day but we were all bored teenagers, sitting indoors. One of them suggested we get out the Ouija board and play with that. I'd done it maybe once or twice before and thought it was harmless fun. Oddly, our skeptical friend thought this was a really bad idea, but never ventured shy he thought that. We got it out and all four sat around the board on the table.

We went through the usual silliness….Great Aunt Tilly (whom no one had ever remembered) contacted us, as did "Zooba-Dooba" the alien. This went around the table as we all took turns asking questions. Slowly, the sun reflecting off the water in the lake, coming through the dappled trees, the monotonous sound of my friends' voices and the warm air, all of this made me sleepy and I felt myself drifting off.

When I started paying attention again, I found myself in a very dark place, but it was warm and I felt safe. I couldn't see or feel anything in front of me, but I had the sensation that there was space around me. After a bit, I began to make out a greyish form some distance off in front of me. It seemed to shimmer and change shape, but it was more or less round. It seemed to grow as well, and then I realized that whatever it was was coming closer. I found this interesting, but I was not threatened by it. Gradually, it grew in size and I could make out more details. It seemed to be a face. Then I realized that I was staring down into water and what I saw was the rippling water changing the appearance of someone's face. I began to feel uncomfortable….I didn't know where I was or how I'd gotten there. The face had no expression at all and was a pale white color. It was coming closer and closer to the surface of the water, which seemed to be very close to my own face. At this point I was beginning to fear this face; I felt as though I were trapped and I wanted to get away. Just as the face was about to break the surface of the water I was jolted awake by my friends. I screamed, which of course made them scream and the board went flying.

I was almost angry at them… "Why didn't you wake me up?! I was having this horrible nightmare!" I told them. They said that really, less than a minute had passed before they realized that my head was slumped forward and I wasn't awake. To me the vision that I saw seemed to have gone on for almost half an hour. I asked them what they had been doing and they said the board spelled out several messages about a boy who had drowned in the lake and that his soul was trapped there. He told them his name, but they only knew of the surname – no one we went to school with had both those names. We wrote the whole experience off to over-active imaginations. Later that summer one of my friends was in town and bumped into a classmate who had the same surname and she told him the strange story of the Ouija board and what her friend had seen while in a trance. He turned ashen and told her that the boy who drowned in the lake was his older brother and since we hadn't gone to school with him we would never have met him.

Nova Scotia, on Canada's east coast was settled by Huguenots from France in the 17th century and they called the region Acadia. When the British defeated the French colonists in New France (now Quebec) in the 1760's, they tried to make the Acadians sign allegiance to the King. They refused, telling the British that they were loyal only to God and so they were expelled from the colonies.

On the north shore of Nova Scotia, my family built a summer cottage on a hill overlooking a beautiful bay, near the foundations of one of these Acadian farms. Spending my summers there I was always regaled with stories of these first European settlers and the tragic events that led to their expulsion. In our area, a British ship was sent to round up the local farmers and fishermen and their families and take them prisoner on the boats which would then take them to Louisiana (hence the term "Cajun" – from Acadia). Usually, these people were pacifists and not inclined to violence or war, but in this case, for some reason they decided once they were on the ship to rebel and try to get back to land. There was a skirmish and the ship caught fire and sank into the ocean, probably killing all the people on board, British and French.

The locals there have for generations passed on stories of seeing the spectral sight of a burning frigate coming up out of the waters at dusk which plies its way across the bay and then sinks back into the dark waters. I'd be told these stories by my grandparents and there is at least one book written on the story. One night, in late summer, just after the sun had set, we were sitting in the cottage when a neighbor told us to go and look out to sea.

My grandfather, father, my brother and myself went outside and we could clearly see this bright red and orange shape rising up out of the water, several miles out to sea. "That's the phantom ship boy!" my grandfather told me. We went down the hill to the beach and for some reason I brought a pair of binoculars. I thought to myself that this was no ghost ship, and for some reason I thought that if I looked at it through the binoculars I wouldn't be able to see it because you can't see ghosts that way, so if I did see something, it must be a real boat in trouble. I don't know why I thought that. I looked at it with the binoculars and oddly enough I could make out the burning sails and rigging and what I thought were people on the decks running around in flames. This shocked me (I was about 13).

The truly odd thing is that all my family who were there that night recanted the story and said it never happened. I chalk that up to their personalities and if something doesn't fit in to their version of reality, they deny or ignore it. One school of thought suggests that it's only the sunset bouncing off refracted light over the horizon, but that doesn't explain what I saw in the binoculars, or why this is only ever seen in this one spot, and not on every seacoast horizon at sunset.

I should preface this next story by saying that I'm an atheist, in that I don't follow any organized religion and I think the ones we have now are merely humankind's need to create order and conformity in the world (or die doing it!). I do believe in the human spirit though, and it is a fact that humans, like all living things, produce and emit electricity and radio waves; both forms of energy. It seems odd to me that this energy would just dissipate when we die. The same might be said for traumatic events in our lives. Maybe those actions leave echoes and imprints long after the places and buildings and people involved have gone. I don't pretend to know the answers to life's mystery or the daily riddles that we are confronted with, only that it's okay not to know all the answers and that every question only leads to more questions, not the solution.

Once I remember falling asleep and thinking about life in general. I was being quiet, I was alone with my thoughts and not distracted by anything or anyone. I remember asking myself what it was all about....*what was the meaning and purpose in life and were we all just alone in this?* I wasn't praying, or even looking for a response, but suddenly I heard this loud booming voice in my head and it said; "You are not alone!"

CHAPTER 47   CLOSING A PORTAL TO THE OTHER SIDE

by Hilary L. Jastram

A friend of mine from high school died. We were not that close but for years I harbored a secret crush on him, while his feelings were not returned. Fast forward decades and I learned he had died. At the time I was heavily into psychics and I would visit one psychic in particular a lot.

When my friend died, I felt in tune with how thin the veil between our worlds is. I had heard strange noises coming from a vent in the corner of my room like a child crying. I had smelled vanilla - and even felt the weight of a hand on my shoulder.

I was open to receive. This was exciting and terrifying at the same time.

One night, I was sitting in my bedroom that had large windows running along the wall. Two sets of curtains hung from the ceiling to the floor. They were heavy and did not move. They did not allow any air to get in. My house was not old, not drafty and my bedroom was pretty cozy.

Suddenly, I felt like I wasn't alone and I took my right hand and put it out to my side, just feeling the air, which was cold. I waved my hand through that chilly spot and when I would pull it back the air was not cold at all. There was an instant change in temperature and I spoke to the spot.

"Hello, is that you, Sheldon?"

And then I yanked my arm back and put it under the cover.

When I talked to the psychic, she told me that what I felt was my friend and the reason that the air was cold was that Sheldon was in the ground and it was frigid there. I told her I was afraid that I had cracked the door to the other side and that other spirits could come through. She told me to go home, sit on my bed and the next time I felt his presence to send him into the light. I felt ridiculous when she said that and as if I was experiencing what it felt like to crack up. She said it wasn't fair to him to keep engaging because when you die before you can be released to inhabit another body that the spirit goes to a spa of sorts. Sheldon was currently immersed in a lavender-scented bath. Or, I had called him out of it. Other souls enter a deep slumber. During these times of rehabilitation, it is selfish of humans missing their people to reach out to the recently departed because it messes up the healing; it pulls them out of their repose.

She told me to take very seriously, what I was about to do, send Sheldon off to resume his journey. He had found me because I was a person who could sense when he was there and he wanted to connect to anyone on this realm, nevermind that I was a distant friend from high school.

I went home and perched on the corner of the bed. I lifted my hand and stirred the air. A cold patch distinctive from the rest of the air in the room had manifested again.

"Sheldon," I said, "you need to go into the light." Then I stopped myself with a chuckle and said under my breath, "And this is how you go crazy."

After a beat, I steeled myself again and said, "I mean it, Sheldon, go into the light. I don't want you here. Don't come back." My voice rose as I said again with a sinking heart: "I don't want you here."

I continued to speak out loud as I slouched over already missing my fading connection with Sheldon while also feeling relieved, "I don't want anything else to be here either. So, whoever you are, I don't want to see you, or sense you, or hear you. Leave me alone!"

After that – no more cold spots, no more smelling scents wafting into the room for no reason. Like a strong scent of vanilla but no one is baking. No more feeling a hand weighing on my shoulder or hearing any sounds coming from the vents. I am bothered infrequently now. I like the peace, but that time also brought me reassurance that there is more after death.

When I was 12 years old, my grandpa died. He had been a clock and watch fixer and delved into some jewelry as well. When he passed, I was given an opal ring, a gold ring and a watch that was so tiny as an adult I could only get my fingers through the silver band. Every once in a while over the years I would take the watch out and look at it. The face is faded and tarnished but the inner and outer workings are so fragile any amount of vigorous cleaning would ruin it. A year ago, after forgetting where I put the watch I found it again and I started talking to my Grandpa Harry and telling him how much I missed him. I began picking up the watch every day and talking to my grandpa a lot and one day, the watch started ticking. I put my ear to it and sure enough, the tiny little mechanisms were clicking along. I hadn't wound it at all!

Shortly after, I misplaced the watch again and didn't think anything of it until my birthday this past year when my husband presented it to me with a new band that had been fashioned by my close friend. My husband had replaced the crystal and I am able to wear it. It functioned for a while until it broke one day and hasn't ticked since. I still wear it anyway to keep Grandpa close.

CHAPTER 48   I KNEW SHE WOULD DIE ON OCTOBER 17

by Randy Spring

Just over two years ago my sister Sharon was in the Oshawa General Hospital fighting lung cancer. I have always had the ability to connect with spirit and know certain things. As for Sharon, I just knew she would die on the 17th of October. I shared this news with my other brothers and sisters weeks before Sharon's passing.

Early morning on October 16th about 8 AM we got the call from the hospital that Sharon's condition was worsening and we may want to come to the hospital. Within the hour all her loved ones were gathered around her.

We all spent the day with her holding her hand just being there - she was in a comatose state so was not responding to any of us. The day soon turned into night. It was a long and draining day. The nurses had brought some cots in the room for us to rest on during the night.

I was laying on the cot when a doctor came in and examined Sharon. After the examination it was about 10 minutes to midnight, the doctor told us to go get a coffee or fresh air because Sharon's vitals were still fairly strong and in no way was her death imminent. As the doctor left, I looked over to my sister lying there so still, and was stunned to see that from nowhere above her head formed a dark cloud. A literal cloud.

Something just told me it was her son Michael who had passed away the previous year coming to meet his mom and guide her to Heaven. I immediately got off the cot and took Sharon's hand. I quietly said to everyone there, "Sharon is ready to go now. Michael is here."

I told Sharon's living son John to come kiss his mom good-bye, which he immediately did. Holding her hand and gently rubbing her cheek, I told Sharon, "I know you can hear me. I know you are ready to leave and Michael is waiting for you. There's nothing to be afraid of. Just keep your faith and go to your son."

Though she was comatose, a tear rolled down her left eye. I knew at this point she could hear everything I was saying. I then continued, "Sharon, at the count of three, we're going to take one final deep breath and you're going to release your soul from your body and join Michael."

I began to count 1, 2, 3… Sharon took one final gasp then one tiny breathe - and she was gone.

My sisters cried out for my brother to go get the doctor to come back in and check her, which he did, saying he was shocked - he thought for sure Sharon would at least lasted till morning.

As things calmed down in the room I looked at the clock on the wall in the room. It was 12.15 AM.

October 17th.

CHAPTER 49   A VOICE SAYS NOT TO REMOVE MY TESTICLES

by Peter

I was diagnosed with cancer four times now. Twice I was scheduled for surgery to remove cancer and each time turned out to be cancer free.

At 27, one day in the shower I noticed a very small hard lump on my left testicle. I told my doctor about it on my next visit to him and he examined me. He put my mind at ease and told me it was just a small epidermoid cyst.

Long story short - over the next 10 years it slowly grew to the size of a small olive. I changed cities a lot when I was young so several doctors had seen this and thought it was a harmless cyst. After moving to a new town I had a visit to my new doc and while examining me he asked about it so I explained that I had been told it was a sub dermal cyst. But he looked concerned and said, "I think we should send you to an oncologist and see what he says."

The oncologist examined me and later in his office he begins to give me instructions to prepare for surgery on Tuesday morning (this was Friday).... Even showed me silicone prosthetics to replace my testicles. I said, "Excuse me, doctor, are you telling me you think I have cancer?" He was very rude and said with sarcasm, almost angry, "Do I THINK you have cancer? I can't believe you let this go so long." I went numb, my mind reeled. He continued with his instructions, "Don't eat or drink after midnight... Here is a prep for painkiller post-surgery... Don't do exercise... "

Then he shows me the prosthetic ball and says I can size up or size down if I want. That he likes to put the prosthetics in right away, unlike some surgeons who put them in after healing which takes two surgeries.

I said, "Them? You're going to remove both my testicles?"

Again his angry sarcastic tone... he says "Come on. You must have done at least basic high school biology. You know the testicles are connected. If there's cancer in one, it's in the other one!"

It was then I heard a voice. It was not in my head... It sounded in the room. It was a deep bass male voice, as if a man was standing a couple of feeT behind the chair I was sitting in. The voice said three times, "No, don't do it." Same pitch and tone each time.

I took the papers and prescriptions the doctor gave me and left. I never went back. This was in the spring and I knew in the fall I was moving to another town, so I decided to listen to the voice and get a second opinion after I moved.

A new doctor in the new town said she thought it was just a hydrocele, a type of swelling in the scrotum that occurs when fluid collects in the thin sheath surrounding a testicle. It's common in newborns and usually disappears without treatment by age one but older boys and adult men can develop a hydrocele from injury or inflammation. She sent me to a surgeon and he said the same thing. Not cancer at all. Nothing to be concerned about.

That Christmas I took a break from school and he did the surgery to make sure. Yes, just a routine hydrocele removal.

Because of that voice I still have both testicles. YAY! I always think it was my guardian angel.

CHAPTER 50 CAN THE TODDLERS SEE THE DEAD MORE CLEARLY?

by Lorrie Fuhriman

My dad passed away at 67 years-old on January 10, 2006, 13 years ago, in White Plains, Kentucky. I am the youngest daughter. I took it really hard. My little three year-old grandson, Zack, didn't like to see me upset or crying so we saved him my tears and did not take him to his great-grandfather's funeral or the burial.

About 3 years before Zack lost his great-grandfather.

One night a week later, Zack had been asleep a couple hours right beside me. As he awoke, he said to me, "Tell Pappy Dude (his name for my dad) to stop touching my finger."

I said, "What do you mean?"

He answered excitedly, "He's here in a fuzzy warm light. It touched my finger."

It was odd to hear this, and I did not know if his imaginations was running wild or what. I asked him what is Pappy Dude wearing? He told me a white shirt with purple and blue stripes. That was exactly what my dad was buried in - that only me and one other person knew because it was a last-minute change!

I asked Zack, "What's he doing now?"

Zack said, "Sitting in the chair watching us."

With mist in my eyes and both a heavy and light heart I looked over to the maroon, gold and blue chair. This was such an unexplainable beautiful moment, but suddenly I worried if my father was in the right place. I rubbed Zack's head and said, "Close your eyes now. Tell him that we are okay and for him to go to the light."

He did, as I held back my tears because little Zack hated when I cried. I whispered, "Do you see him now?"

He whispered back, "No, he's gone now."

I still have that old chair and cannot part with it. I will never forget that last visit from my dad. I have a Red 13 tattoo on my hand because his handle on CB radio was Red 13. Also carved into me is a line from the song I had played for him at his funeral, "How do I go on?"

Dad, I guess the answer is with faith because you have shown us there is indeed an afterlife.

CHAPTER 51   MIRACULOUSLY SAVED FROM DEATH CRASH

by Dennis Headrick

The difficulty of growing up gay forty years ago in an ultra-conservative Pentecostal home isn't a unique story. All that makes mine stand out is because it's my story and how I finally came to know, in spite of everything I'd been raised to believe, that God or a higher power loves me and accepts me just as I am - as queer as I am.

My first, and perhaps my greatest love, was a boy in our church. His name was Charlie. And I know that Charlie loved me. The backstory of Charlie and I is a whole other tale, but for the purposes of this book, I'll just say he left me and the church because of a sexual encounter we had. I was devastated. I held myself, I know now unfairly, wholly to blame for his departure. Especially his exodus from the faith. You know the passage, "Verily I say unto you, Inasmuch as ye have done it unto one of the least of these my brethren, ye have done it unto me."

I had failed my God, my brother, and the love of my life. I believed I did not deserve to live. Still trying desperately to hold onto some remnant of my faith, on a stormy Saturday night I headed out to a young people's meeting at a Pentecostal church in Dallas. The entire way I sobbed, ravaged with shame and praying for some kind of absolution.

I had the radio tuned to a gospel music station. Torrential rain plummeted, obscuring all sight. Other cars had pulled off beside the interstate to wait for some cessation of the flooding roadway. Halfway between my hometown of Hillsboro and Dallas there are double bridges, one each side of the divided interstate, crossing a medium sized creek. The access roads on either side "U" under the bridges which, of course, are supported by massive concrete pillars.

I wanted to die, but I knew my mother would barely if at all survive my suicide. Approaching the bridge on the northbound side of I-35, I saw a way out. "Why not?", I wondered. "They'll just think it was a terrible accident, and I'm damned to Hell anyway." And so, I did it.

I veered off the road and headed down the cement embankment (it was about a 75 foot drop). When my front tires hit the few feet of grass before the next cement highway, my car began an end-on-end tumble. Down I went, somehow avoiding the pillars, like a daredevil skier that was plunging head over heels... but in a vehicle weighing a ton. At the bottom, what was left of my car flipped once more, hitting the U section of the access roads - and landed beyond them, upside down, in the creek that had swollen to a rushing river because of the storm.

I found myself seat belted in what was effectively a metal box (or in this case most probably a coffin) upside down and water was rushing in. The water didn't have far to go, only inches, before I'd drown. I was panicked! Crazy! I screamed out, "OH GOD! I wanted to die... but I DON'T WANT TO DROWN LIKE THIS!"

That's all I remember until, somehow, I found myself back at the road and someone, he had an ethereal quality - a ghostly aura - was reaching down to take my hand and lift me up beside the road.

Here's the kicker, or at least one of the kickers... he said to me, "God loves you just as you are. God made you who you are. Everything will be alright."

Wow! How the heck did he know??? I sat down by the pavement (the rain had abated somewhat), and when I looked up he was gone. Just... gone.

It wasn't five minutes before the ambulance arrived. This was before cellphones and there was no place (a service station or other) to use a phone for miles, so how they got a call to come and get me, I've no idea. I didn't have a scratch or bruise!

The police later asked when I was thrown out of the car. I explained, tried to explain, that I hadn't been... that I was in the car upside down when it hit the water. They insisted that was impossible because, amazingly, all the windows on the vehicle were intact! - the engine was in the passenger seat, and the trunk against the back of the front seats. It was, indeed a metal box with NO POSSIBLE EXIT.

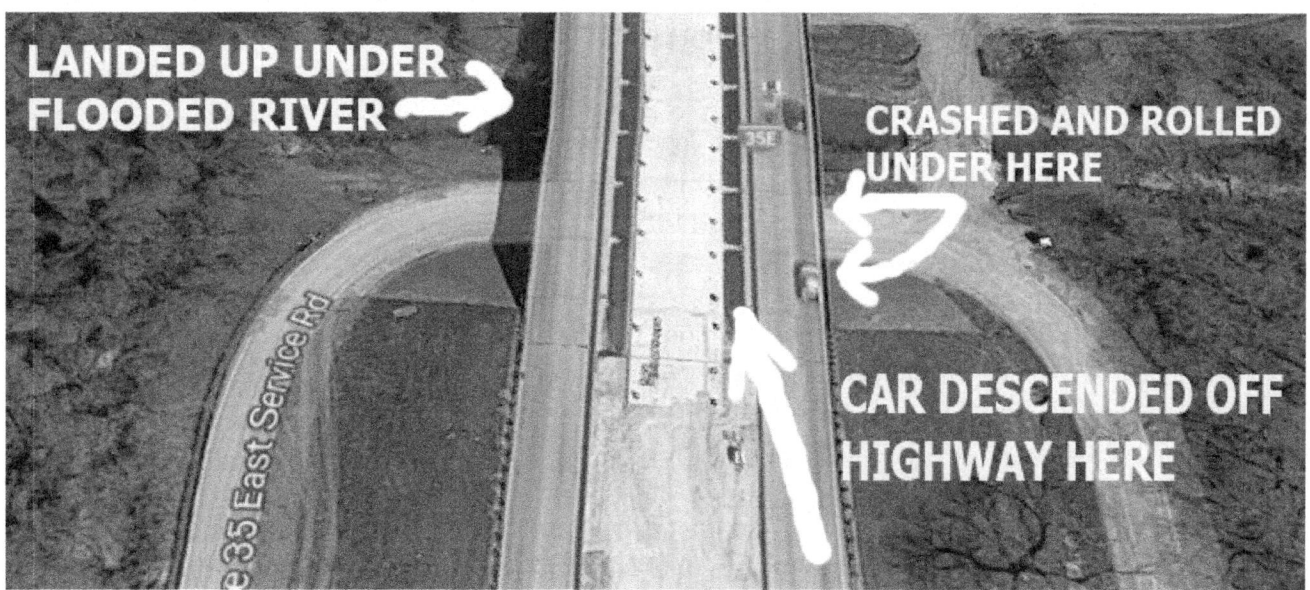

But I know, without a doubt, that I was in that car when the car landed in the water. And these other things I've known since... that was no ordinary man that somehow knew my darkest secret and also this... that God loves me and made me just the way I am.

I'm sending you two google map views of the interstate where the bridges are... a long view and a closer view. Because the 135 has to cross the Waxahachie Creek as well as the access roads that "U," the bridge(s) had to be elevated. Just before them is the typical grassy area dividing the northbound (I was traveling north to Dallas) and southbound (it goes on to Austin and Corpus Christi). But a few feet beyond the interstate's pavement they paved the steep embankment with cement down to the "U" beyond which is the creek.

The car hit the rain soaked grass and began its tumble end-over-end down over the cemented area, over the "U," and landed upside down in the creek. One of the arguments I had with the police was if I'd been thrown out of the car onto the cement embankment, wouldn't I have had physical evidence - cuts/bruises, broken bones, etc.? They just couldn't believe I escaped the car in the creek ...

I can't believe it either, but somehow it happened.

It's been more than 40 years. Here's where I left the road. Again... That center construction wasn't there. It was just the two bridges. Also... "75 foot" was a guesstimate. Looking at this I'm thinking it was much a much longer trip. The incline down between the bridges is very steep, and then there's the service roads before the Waxahachie Creek.

I don't claim to have many (if any) answers. I do believe this, and only this: that evening there was a miraculous intervention meant only to alleviate my guilt, desire to end my life, and give me a sense that my homosexuality was not "sinful" but, like my blond hair and hazel eyes, just another facet of who I am - who I was born to be. And it did the trick. I've not had a moment of guilt about Charlie or my sexuality since. It was, without a doubt, the most life-changing experience in my life.

CHAPTER 52   EXITING BANKING FOR A SPIRITUAL LIFE

by Carl Moellenberg

As you know, my life took a wonderful and very different mid-life turn. I started out working in the financial arena for firms such as Morgan Stanley, Goldman Sachs and ultimately was Chief of Staff to the President of Chemical Bank (which is now Chase). Then after some time, I decided I needed to exercise the creative side of my brain and turned to producing on Broadway and more recently film. I have never been happier; telling incredible stories which transform people and impact their lives is very important to me. I've been lucky to win 10 Tony awards to date by finding such projects that really touch audiences.

This career turn was not totally surprising because my first love has always been music. I studied classical piano and sang in several classical singing groups before my financial career. It was just a matter of time to get back to it. Musical theater was the choice for me to be intimate with music again.

However, when I exited investment banking, I could not immediately wave my hand and say "Now I am a producer." There was much to learn, mentors to find, training from the Broadway League, etc.. In that gap period of time, I also explored my spiritual side. Investment banking had extremely long hours and there was no opportunity to have a life outside of that. I traveled extensively around the world and also enrolled in several healing schools and modalities. I took classes in Swedish and Shiatsu bodywork. I became a Reiki master and learned to understand energy over a two year training period. I also, after graduating from another school, became ordained as minister. I counseled at walk-in clinics for homeless people and online for gay youth. I talked one on one for six months with a shaman who had studied from healers in Peru. This time period felt blessed, calm, serene and opened my eyes to what is truly important in life.

The single event, however, that I will NEVER forget is on the day I was ordained at the third healing school. It was a bright, sunny and warm spring day. The event took place in midtown and I decided to walk about 30 blocks to my home in Chelsea. As I started walking down Fifth Avenue on this gorgeous day, I looked to my left and saw a small bright gold bird that certainly did not seem like it remotely belonged in NYC. I have never seen a bird like that here ever since and it reminded me of Caribbean birds.

This bird decided to partly walk and partly fly next to me down the entire length of Fifth Avenue. It would walk a bit and then fly to catch up with me and then wait until I had pulled level, block by block. I was in awe of what was happening! Many other people on the streets were equally amazed and stopped to essentially gawk at this bird. I got to 25th Street, where I had to turn right to get to Seventh Avenue. I literally stopped and told the bird that I needed to turn here. The bird looked at me for a bit and then flew right at me, grazing my hair and then flying off.

I talked to my teacher and several other friends when I arrived home, because I was stunned by this occurrence. My teacher told me that he believed a higher being sent the bird to tell me that I had a calling and a reason to follow this path in helping others. I completely think my golden bird escort was a welcome to a spiritual world for me.

There are always signals out there which lead us to what truly matters — loving and connecting to others in a meaningful way.

CHAPTER 53 THOM BIERDZ'S OTHER PSYCHIC EXPERIENCES

by Thom Bierdz

In chapter 1 it was explained my compulsion to create this book was because of the 9/11 premonition seeing thousands of light entities flying into a dark tunnel of hurt, and I wanted to close with a summary of my many other paranormal events.

Even as a child I knew life continued beyond our Earthly plane, but cannot recall one specific enlightening event which triggered this belief. Raised Catholic, but casually so; not like any of us actually read the Bible, we just went to church when our Italian mom made us go; sometimes weekly, more often monthly. Fidgeting in the uncomfortable wood pews, my little mouth buttoned shut and my brown eyes enlarged, darting between the dramatic Biblical statuary and the handsome priests. Being a gay boy in the 1960's when religious people condemned homosexuals to Hell, for my own safety I began to distance myself from most the finger-wavers who attended St. Marks in Kenosha, Wisconsin. I have since then been wary of structure, conformity and tradition. My God loved me completely, I felt, and He must approve of me, despite my "evil" masturbating, because I was a very good-intentioned polite straight-A student.

My belief in a god with a white beard dissipated over time, but throughout each of my 56 years, my spiritual seeking matched the passion of my sexual fervor. Exploring over a dozen wonderful monogamous relationships, and just as many new-age gurus, I have finally arrived at the exact same metaphysical belief systems leading this age of consciousness. Though I have never had a Near Death Experience, there are hundreds shared on YouTube, and they eloquently articulate the same "truths" I lock into now: we humans have been given the gift of the gods, to create our lives, our energy attracts similar energy, our vibrations attract similar vibrations, law of attraction, love over fear, no one will judge us but us - after death we will experience the emotions of everyone we encountered, and judge ourselves (to gain compassion and grow).

Please understand that my belief system totally substantiates yours, whatever it is. I sincerely believe that anything you believe is in fact true, for you. People can exist cohesively while in different realities.

I believe our human experience can be reduced to consciousness and light (*The Secret Of Light* by

Walter Russell) and in this play-station not only can we become deliberate creators (Esther Hicks / AbrahamHicks.com) but what is "true" varies to the person. It seems to me at this point that if you die and BELIEVE Jesus will greet you, He will. Same with Buddha or Allah, or even Shirley MacLaine or Marlon Brando. WhatEVER one believes is true for them. I personally think of god now as quite different from the jealous, punishing Bible archetype and apart from the white-bearded paternal guide who loved me unconditionally as a clumsy child. Today I'd say that god can be defined as the limitless unified field of potentiality – allowing each of us unencumbered creation.

I always felt spirits around me and did have a few unexplainable paranormal happenings as a child. One night I awoke in my dark bedroom experiencing colonial dancers twirling right through my very body. Everything was black but they were all outlined in light. Terrified, I screamed for Dad to rescue me, and he came downstairs to comfort me, but looking back, I wonder if I slipped into a previous incarnation? - or maybe even time-travel? Nevertheless my fear shut it off and it never repeated.

As a teen I wondered if I could/should be a channel, and successfully did psychic readings with normal playing cards at school recesses – but as a young man in Hollywood rerouted my focus to auditions and the material pursuits of capitalism.

A hundred million people worldwide embraced me as the vulnerable teen Phillip Chancellor III on *The Young and the Restless* from 1986-1989 (and I reappeared in 2004 and 2009-2011). It was a huge ego trip to be paid thousands of dollars and flown to malls and sign autographs for throngs of screaming girls, but I left my three-year contract hoping to become a Hollywood movie star. That never happened but I did okay earning many small TV parts.

As decades passed, my creative drive pushed me to write and paint, which brought many awards. My first memoir, *Forgiving Troy,* detailed my journey to forgive my paranoid schizophrenic brother for murdering our wonderful mom – forgiveness which only happened because of a very specific psychic message I received from my dead mother (that will be after this chapter). (Netflix's *Evil Lives Here* interviewed me for a recent episode titled "The Soap Star's Secret" which highlighted many of the events in *Forgiving Troy.)*

Before that 1994 event which led me back to forgive my brother in prison, I had been obsessed for nearly five years trying to reach my dead mother.

Though I tried to reach her directly week after week, month after month, seeing psychic after psychic, I got few results. True that James Van Praagh delivered exactly the words I asked Mom to say, but a dozen other psychics did not impress me with their predictable generalizations. Slowly though, with deliberate effort, I did experience some contact.

Several times when I was calling out to her from my bed I felt her comforting weight shifting on the covers. I did not have any indoor pets at that time. This happened even in the light.

Other times she came to me in dreams. But a few times the dreams became visits – and there is a huge difference! In the visits, either seeing or hugging her, I was no longer asleep. I had awakened, startled from her presence. This brought powerful love and tears, and though it can be dismissed by doubters as imagined, we who have had the visitations know the reality of them.

Me in my 20's.

One day in a restaurant I actually saw my deceased mother. Not like I mistook someone who looked like her – because Mom was not completely visible in the way the customers were – but Mom was just as real and layered over the others. No, I was not drinking, and I'll further chance embarrassment by telling you it was at Sizzler. I know it sounds ridiculous, but it IS funny, and Mom and I have a good sense of humor, but Mom was not laughing in this apparition. She was waving to me to get my attention. But the most heartfelt part of the happening was how happy she was. That is what I took away, which issued me great relief.

Though I could never hear any words directly from her spirit and she never came through in any of our séances, my friends were pleased a matchstick bent.

There was also the time an electrical cord tapped me, waking me as I slept on the loft mattress. It startled me awake and I examined it in the light, as the sun shined through a near large window, but there was no logical reason for that poltergeist activity. There were no bugs or rodents near who could have moved it. Something supernatural moved it.

Another time, after I started to forgive Troy in prison, three finger taps to my head awoke me. Again I was in the loft alone. Because this entity got me up. Two minutes later I was downstairs, in the dark before the sun came up, just in time to answer the ringing phone, which I would have ignored had I been sleeping. That morning my brother Troy called from prison to express remorse of killing Mom for the first time. I believe Mom really wanted to make sure I got that call.

Another time I felt a hand shake my shoulder three times to awake me. I don't know why.

Probably over twenty times I have awaken shaking or trembling, but it feels like the bed is shaking or trembling. My guess is I had just crashed into my body from astral travels, though I do not recall them.

If I try hard I can see a white aura around anything, and only once saw a yellow aura around a man. I have no idea what that meant. I do focus on attracting only positive psychic phenomena and run from anything demonic or frightening…

…like the time some friends and I went to investigate an older outlandish character named Don Blythe in what appeared to be an average ranch-style house in El Monte, California. It was anything but ordinary. Don generously shared everything in his museum-like home with us, showing us mummies, something resembling a vampire, what looked like a miniature space alien and jars containing cyclops and brain tumors and Siamese twins and mermaids. When he touched our young friend, Veronica, on her elbow, blood appeared. I could've spent all day there but my boyfriend got us out quick and convinced me not to go back for the séance that was offered.

Back on December 12, 1993, I had an Out Of Body experience. My boyfriend and I were visiting an older couple who were teachers of *The Science Of Mind*, which was enthralling me to dreams of levitation – which probably spurred on an actual OOB that night. As we went to bed, I literally rose from my body and flew out the window and arrived in some beautiful park and was introduced to my spirit guide. He told me his name but I feel it's too personal (and inconsequential) to share, and after much adventure and conversation, which I have forgotten, he said if I ever told anyone about the OOB it would never happen again. I told. It never happened again. (!!)

Not long after, my boyfriend and I visited his family in Michigan. We took his mom to her weekly Bingo. What a strange coincidence that I sat next to a woman named Phyllis (my mom's name) who had a son named Troy (my brother's name – the one who killed Mom)! How many Phyllis's have sons named Troy? What are the odds I would be conversing with one about this, and then, for the first and only time in my life, had an absolute knowing I was soon to win the $500 black-out prize which was about to start. I gulped nervously, dobbing my Bingo card as numbers were called, with much social anxiety because all these people wanted to win and here was a soap opera star going to take the night's big prize. I felt guilty. Let me make clear I did not THINK I would win. I KNEW with absolute certainty in a minute I would yell, "Bingo," and so I practiced in my head exactly how to announce it without looking like a panic attack. Claiming the prize with trepidation, and gratitude, I split the winnings with my boyfriend's mother. Living in a trailer she sure appreciated it.

Though I have spent hundreds of hours in Vegas casinos since, never again did I get this knowingness I would win. Weird that I had a knowing I would win the jackpot but did not hear an actual voice say that. I have only heard an actual voice a few times. I am assuming it is a spirit but cannot tell if I hear it outside or inside my head. Once it told me a word – so I looked it up and found it was a vitamin – so I have taken it since! And once I was very aggravated at a beeping sound in my house. It was driving me crazy and I had no idea what it was. After searching every cupboard, I heard a voice say, very clearly, "It's usually on the ceiling." What the heck is usually on the ceiling? You may have figured out already it was a fire alarm but this was about 1990 and I was new to fire alarms and new to that house and I didn't know fire alarms beeped when they were low on batteries. But because of the voice, in the back of the pantry, near the floor I found the beeping fire alarm and removed the batteries to finally get silence.

Sometimes when I closed my eyes I saw a grainy film-strip on one side and I was in another location, like the backseat of a car. I wonder if I was accessing another person's mind? I would see things through their eyes – literally. Usually in black and white, or black with white outlines, I see their moving point of view. It has happened more regularly lately and I wonder if as a child when I saw white-outlined colonial dancers that somehow my consciousness was transported back hundreds of years, seeing that event through someone else's eyes as it was happening. Occasionally on that same brain channel I find myself watching military activity as it is happening – in blackness, I perfectly see the figures and objects outlined in white / light / electricity / aura.

Another miraculous occurrence was the time I fell at a gym, crashing my head to steel, and was paralyzed. Never before or again have I experienced paralysis, but as my body lay dead, I was conscious. I felt no pain and had no feeling in my body whatsoever. My body could not move, but my eyes could, and I glanced to the side to see if anyone would help me. My thoughts were not affected or stifled or unclear, but my mouth could not move to scream. *Oh. My. God. I thought, I really did it this time, but NOOOOOOOOO!! I was not going to be paralyzed!!* Flashing through my head were my recent victimization thoughts, like *I am supposed to be a big star and I am tired of trying so hard and being rejected on auditions. Just fast forward to my destined fame, damn it!!* It occurred to me that I was getting what I asked for—and had created an opportunity to be asleep, or paralyzed, until my desired fame happened. *Nooooooo!! my thoughts screamed. I will NOT BE PARALYZED!! NOOO!! I will not allow it!* Within five more minutes, I could rise - and walked out of the gym. I was convinced I had created an opportunity for paralysis, but my will canceled it.

After 28 years of auditions, I left Hollywood. As an empath, the over-stimulus ate at me 24/7 and I craved an escape. Eventually surrendering my movie-star dreams in my mid-life crisis at 49, I found peace painting portraits from a mountain cottage in Lake Arrowhead, California. Burnt out on crowds in Los Angeles for so many years, I relished the seclusion to explore spirituality, become vegan and raise rescues dogs. Five years ago I did attempt to give psychic readings over the phone to Facebook fans, and half said I was right on but half said I was way off. This was important feedback because even though my belief that I could be a purposeful medium existed since I was a child, fine-tuning was still needed to decipher what images and words were meant for the client and which were the rambling filings of my subconscious meant only for me. Not like I made stuff up – there was no shortage of symbols bouncing in my head – I just did not know who they belonged to…

Now that I finished my second memoir, *Young, Gay & Restless*, and analyzed 50 years of patterns in my amusing sex life, I will my focus to be on contacting spirits who can help evolve our species and end unnecessary suffering across the planet.

I pay my bills painting portraits from photos sent to me, which is certainly an effort, but I feel my best artwork is the casual expressionism that spilled from my subconscious. Some were shown throughout this book as Tarot-like cards; my 100 BLUE X paintings (BLUE X from two crossing blue lines: Earth plane and above. Something above was directing my paintbrush in these; I "knew" to put a specific shape on top right, etc., and I just followed the orders until they stopped, then sat back and thought, "Wow, okay,

I can see aspects of my life patterns and dramas, but most of this is probably meant for others?"

About a year after painting these in 2015, it occurred to me to make these a deck like Tarot cards, and the matching text flew out of me, channeled by a higher source.

Psychic stuff had happened in my earlier paintings as well. About ten years ago, frustrated I could not get a man's boot in a horse's stirrup to look right, after so many attempts, I just said aloud, angry, "Okay you do it!" and I watched as the brush used white instead of black. This made no sense to me at all. Nevertheless, I let it continue going in a new direction and the bottom of the boot emerged, not the side which I was trying to make fit. The shiny bottom was exactly what the leg angle needed. A higher source completed the boot perfectly!

In the below painting I did around 2010 for a FB friend who commissioned me to paint his sister with her recently deceased husband, something told me to paint roses. Afterward, I asked the client if that improvised addition was okay and he was floored, saying, "Dave gave Shirley 5 roses on the 5th day of every month because they were married on the 5th!"

Why had I felt compelled to paint roses – and exactly 5?! As if that wasn't enough of a message from the afterlife, a few minutes later I was totally freaked out discovering this image had miraculously become my screen saver. It was not at my doing - and no other human was around. Dave obviously wanted to reach out to his beloved, grieving wife. Was that why I also felt compelled to paint an envelope, a symbol of communication?

In 2004 I put a canvas on the floor, leaned over it, and said, "God, I want to paint your face today!" About an hour later I had finished the landscape, disappointed God did not take over my brush and paint his essence in the clouds. It was close a few times on the left, but looked contrived, so I just gave up. Later I noticed a blue face with black mustache and beard that I had not consciously painted in the sky! - On the right!

"Where did this face come from?!" I gasped, then was embarrassed because it looked more like me than God. How hedonistic! However, as the years passed and my spiritual journey progressed, I no longer believed God had a specific human face, rather god to me had become a unified field of potentiality allowing everything to exist. Just this year, creating this chapter, I realized my current beliefs dictate that I am god and you are god and your mom is god, etc.. Years before painting MY face as the face of god embarrassed me - but now it makes perfect sense because I stated, "God, I want to paint your face today!" For me, I AM the face of god. For you, YOU are the face of god.

I think you are limitless.

CHAPTER 54 MY DEAD MOM DEMANDS I SEE TROY, HER KILLER

by Thom Bierdz with Gary Scheuerman

Although I have been fortunate enough to have much spirit contact which was itemized in the previous chapter, this next spirit message changed my life, and may have saved my brother's soul. This is Chapter 30 from my first memoir, *Forgiving Troy*.

The Message - 1994

[My ex, Cowboy] Gary and I talked at least once a year to share what was new in our lives. I'd called him in 1993 when I got acting job – playing a murderer in an episode of *Matlock*. We also discussed how I was settling into a "routine" life with [boyfriend] Big Dog at his condo in Valley Village, half-an-hour north of Hollywood.

Gary phoned to tell me when he quit bar tending and bought a quiet ranch above Green Bay in Door County wilderness. He lived there with a hot Wisconsin cowboy of his own named Scott. During the summer they ran a restaurant in the high-tourist area. The only time they really had to see people was during the four warm months of the year when their restaurant was open. Other than that, they had their horses and dogs to keep them busy, and lots of wood to chop.

The last time Gary called, he was concerned because he had a vision of his German Shepherd getting hit by a truck. When he phoned in January of 1994, I was afraid he'd tell me this premonition had come true. But it was another premonition he was calling about – a more frightening premonition – and it was for me.

Gary was weeping over the phone, which was very out of character for someone so masculine. He was embarrassed, but couldn't stop himself.

"I've got to talk to you, TJ," he wailed, "I've got a message for you."

"A message?"

"I'm not sure who it's from…I think it's your mother's soul, but it could be a part of your brother's soul – or some weird combination. I'm in pain, real pain."

"I can hear that in your voice. Pain where?"

"I've never felt anything like it," Gary continued laboriously. "It's excruciating… I'm on the floor, curled over. I can't stand it."

He wept for almost a full minute. "It's horrible! You can't imagine – it's not human–"

"Shit, Gary, I'm sorry…"

"I'm supposed to feel…this…pain…to…show you…to convince…you of…their pain."

"Whose pain?"

"Theirs, I think. I don't know, hers or his or a combination, like I said, but it's all wrong. It's so fucked up," he groaned louder.

I listened to Gary vomit. Finally he returned.

"Teej, I'm supposed to tell you that your mother loves you very much. 'Her four'… she keeps saying 'she loves her four.'"

"I know she loves us kids," I breathed into the phone, emotional. I felt my mother near. Goosebumps layered my arms.

"You have to save him!" Gary demanded.

"Who?"

"Oh, Teej, man, Troy's soul is… damn it!… dying."

"Troy's soul? In prison?"

"Yes. Yes. Troy is in trouble. She wants you to go to him."

"No way."

"You're the only one who can save him," he said. "She keeps saying that. His soul. It's urgent. These five years have devastated him, I guess. You have to go to him now."

Troy and Mom in happier times.

I didn't say anything for quite a while as Gary repeated his words over and over. Gary did not know I'd been pleading to my mother in prayer, begging her to speak to me. Reflecting on my selfish relationship with her, I wanted to make it up to her and had been asking her if there was anything I could do for her. I had been calling on her spirit for almost five years.

"I need some time to think about this," I told Gary, coldly.

"She keeps saying you have to go. Now. If you could feel this pain."

"Why me?"

"She says you're the only one. Do it for her, she's begging you."

After a long beat, Gary calmed himself. "The message is complete," he sighed, grateful.

"Gary, Troy severed any connection to me, to our whole family, when he killed her. As far as I'm concerned, he is dead and that's great."

"His soul is dying."

"Souls don't die," I argued.

"I never thought about that, about souls dying. I honestly hadn't," Gary said. "But she said it, they said it kind of together."

"When something dies it transforms itself, even science proves that. So an energy – Troy's – whatever it is – cannot stop. Right?"

"That's not what the message says," Gary reiterated, "Don't underestimate what just happened. I didn't ask for this. It was huge, man. The biggest thing that's ever happened to me in my life. This was a message from some very strange place."

"I believe you," I explained, "I know you."

No one in the family had maintained contact with Troy in the past four and a half years, and they expected to keep it that way. But after hearing Gary for half-an-hour on the phone, I could see there was no way to refuse him and avoid seeing Troy. The more adamantly he insisted I see Troy, the more terrified I became of that possibility. Troy had been as dead to our family emotionally, as we had prayed he were physically. If Troy was not dead, and Gary's message seemed to say he was not, wouldn't Troy be a hardened bully in a prison gang, probably killing inside those walls? He had lifted weights, and his years in Tae Kwon Do class probably assured him a place in the prison hierarchy, so why the fuck was I supposed to visit him? I mean, what was Troy really like now – in 1994? Why did Mom want me to go to him? It didn't make any sense.

That night, in between nightmares of being murdered, I lay awake tossing. In the past five years, and for the next decade to come, to the chagrin of every boyfriend I had, I couldn't sleep at night for more than two hours in a row.

The next morning while Big Dog nervously paced, I phoned the Columbia Correctional Prison and talked to Admittance to check out the situation. The person on the phone said he had to send an officer to Troy, who was housed in the psychiatric unit, to get his permission to see me. On TV shows, I had seen visitors face prisoners with thick glass between them. That thought comforted me slightly, but still I wondered what does Troy have to lose by using his black belt skills to break through the glass and attack me? He was already sentenced to life in prison. He had made it clear that he hated me, and could now deliver on his threat to rip out my heart in six seconds and hold it in front of my face until I died.

Was it because he and I looked more alike than any others in the family? Was he still jealous of my past success? Was he even more threatened by my homosexuality? Did his hate grow, because, like our mother, I intervened – and even had him live under my roof, and insisted he follow my rules – in expectation of him maturing?

If Troy finally decided to act on his threats, I would be dead unless the guards took less than six seconds to draw their guns and fire.

Big Dog pleaded with me not to go. As much as I loved him, I was very independent and not about to listen to him. Our relationship was a case of opposites attracting, and I didn't include him in on much of my life because he simply wouldn't understand it.

Neither would [my other brother] Gregg. When I told him about the message, he didn't believe it. He said I deserved to die if I did something as stupid as seeing Troy.

I received the prison's clearance to visit. I also received Troy's indirect permission through Mike Grove, one of the prison's psychiatric counselors. For my safety, I requested Mike be present when I saw Troy.

Ignoring Big Dog's anxious concern, I reserved a flight for January 16. My return flight would be twenty-four hours later. I decided that was plenty of time to land in Milwaukee, rent a car, drive to the middle of Wisconsin, and see Troy.

100 Black And White Male Nude Prints &
100 Black And White Photos Of The Artist
Thom Bierdz
100 Black And White Male Nude Prints
Thom Bierdz
& 100 Black And White Photos Of The Artist

THE BLUE X CARDS + 200 Divination Readings
Thom Bierdz
COMPASSION
ROAD RAGE
48
PASSENGER
THE ALIEN
BLANK CANVAS
12
BEGIN AGAIN
TRUTH
GUILT
46
THE BLUE X CARDS
+200 Divination Readings
VORTEX
96
FREEDOM
15
JUSTICE
LOSS
JOURNEY
SEER
INHERITANCE
CHANGE THE PAST
SOULMATE
Thom Bierdz
?

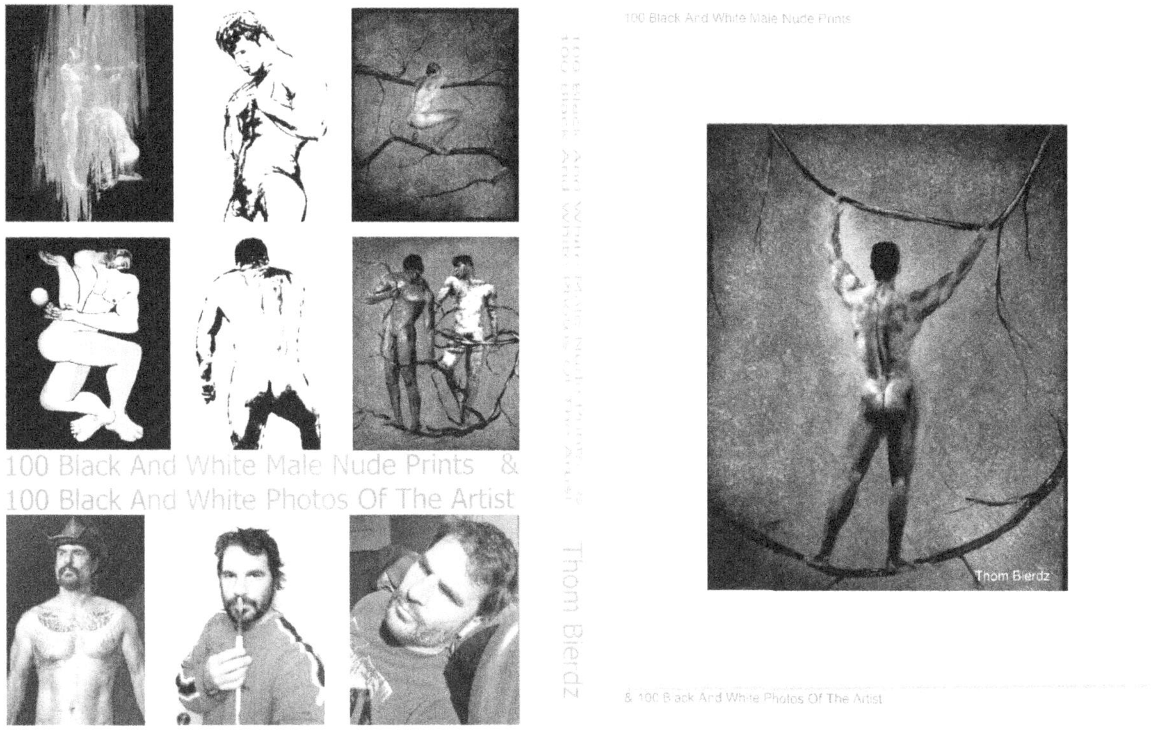

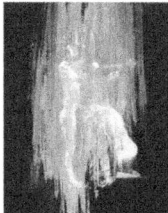

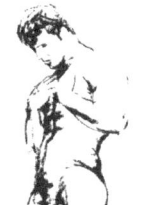

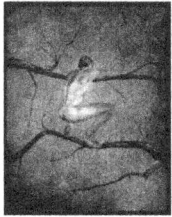

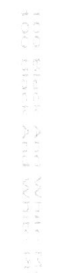

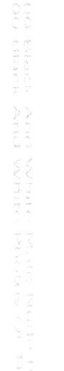

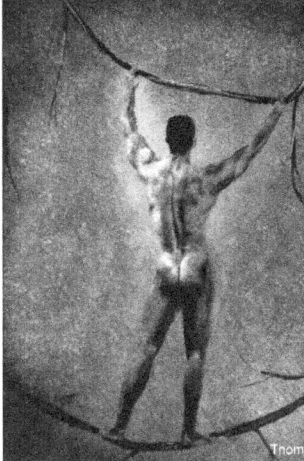

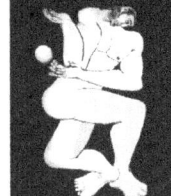

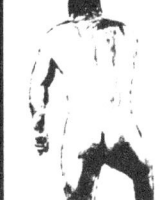

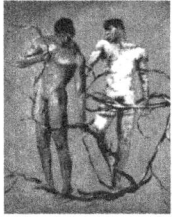

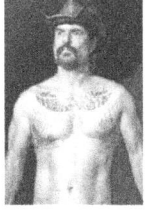

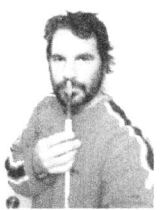

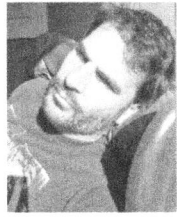

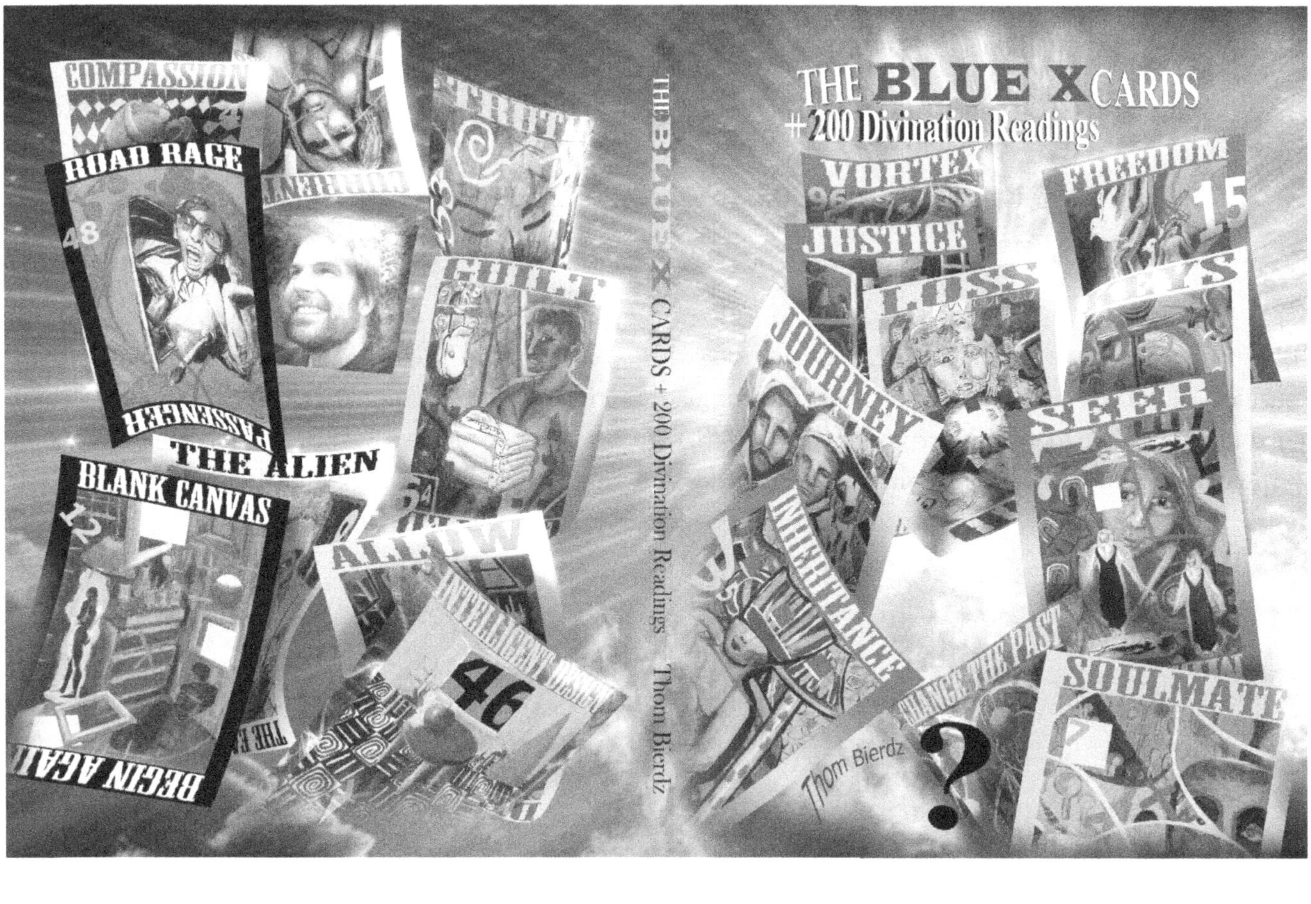

If you want YOUR miraculous spirit account in

THEY WANT TO HELP US: VOLUME TWO

contact Thom Bierdz at Facebook or **at** www.ThomBierdz.com

Want more miracles?

Maybe *THE BLUE X PAINTINGS + 200 Divination Readings* is the answer.

EBook, paperback and hardcover info

on all of Thom's books

at www.ThomBierdz.com

"Bierdz marries an innate flair for composition with a compulsion for seriality delivering aesthetically engaging patterned art which is at the same time both primitive and complex. The echoing of shapes illustrates how human events derive into one another. In his unique style, he pushes the language of current spiritual exploration forward, spinning form and content, questioning scale and the creation of each moment, offering innovative and inspiring work on par with Picasso, Van Gogh, Matisse and Warhol," HIGHLIGHT HOLLYWOOD, Tommy Lightfoot Garrett.

"Bierdz is able to paint on that instinctual level." GENRE MAGAZINE, Mitch Rustad.

"Bierdz is now one of Los Angeles' most successful and in-demand artists." EXPRESS NEWS, David Alexander Nahmod.

Made in United States
Orlando, FL
03 June 2024

47493914R10102